You

God

Youthwork and the Mission of God

Frameworks for Relational Outreach

PETE WARD

First published in Great Britain 1997
Society for Promoting Christian Knowledge
Holy Trinity Church
Marylebone Road
London NW1 4DU

British Library Cataloguing-in-Publication Data

A catalogue record of this book is available from
the British Library

ISBN 0–281–05044–9

Data manipulation by David Gregson Associates,
Beccles, Suffolk
Printed in Great Britain by The Cromwell Press,
Melksham, Wiltshire

To Mike Riddell and Mark Pierson

CONTENTS

Contents

PREFACE

I HAVE TWO people to thank for the inspiration to set pen to paper. In 1996 I was very kindly invited to visit New Zealand/Aotearoa by Mike Riddell and Mark Pierson. Mike arranged for me to deliver the Lanyon Lectures at Carey College in Auckland. The notes from these lectures and the week of sessions I prepared for students at the college form the backbone of this present book. I am happy to dedicate this book to Mike and Mark who made an incredible trip both memorable and, above all, great fun.

I also should thank all the people who have been kind enough to invite me to speak at conferences and training events during the last three years. The fact that I have incorporated most of my talks into the material in this book means that I will now have to think of something new to say. A fact which I know will come as a relief to many.

Pete Ward
Oxford

INTRODUCTION

THE STORY OF this book is really the story of my own ministry with young people. In 1980 I was employed by St Michael's Church in Macclesfield. My job title was 'lay missioner' and I was employed to work as an itinerant musician. This meant that I travelled around the country doing concerts and taking part in missions. Schools seemed to be the place for the aspiring Christian singer/songwriter at that time and I would often find myself alongside a Scripture Union worker taking lessons and assemblies for unsuspecting pupils in places such as Middlesborough or Hull.

Three years of this work left me with two convictions: I wanted to stop travelling around; and there had to be a better way of reaching out to young people than short-term, one-off missions. I solved the first problem by taking a job with St Clement's Church in Oxford. Here my role was to run the church-based youth group and to play an active part in the life of the congregation. (Being active seemed to involve quite a lot of chair moving as far as I could see.) My first idea in this new job was that I would try and take what I had learned from travelling around the country and apply it in my local situation. So along with other church youthworkers I set about running a school-based mission in the Oxford area. The plan was that in each church there would be an evangelistic coffee bar and these would be publicized through assemblies and lunch-time events at the local school nearest to each of our churches. In this way we planned to run two or three coffee bars in different parts of the city.

The plan was excellent and it worked very well in the churches where there was a good-sized, lively youth group. In the church I attended, however, we only had a very small group. This meant that we did not have a wide network of friendships amongst the young people which I could see was the basis for success in the other churches in town. Looking back at the situation in our own church I am sure that a more experienced youthworker would have taken a lot more time to build up the existing group making sure that they were confident in themselves and their faith before setting out on a mission.

I should explain the person who has had the most influence over my work amongst young people is an American called Arnie Jacobs. I met Arnie for the first time when I started my job at St Clement's. On my first day in the parish I found that Arnie had been booked to speak at the fellowship meeting. Of course I had been around a bit and felt I knew it all and there was no way that an American, least of all one in his sixties, was ever going to teach me anything. As I listened Arnie talked about the way that Jesus changed people's lives through relationships. He spoke about the need young people had for friendship with adults and how this could lead them to faith.

From my experience I knew that what Arnie was saying was true. I had seen young people changed while I had been visiting schools around the country. The problem was I could recall occasions where my heart had ached as we drove away in the van, and I could see no way that these young people would ever connect up with a local church. I had moved to Oxford precisely for this reason. Hit-and-run evangelism had left me searching for a better way.

Arnie worked for an organization in the United States called Young Life and he was generous enough to invite me to come and stay with him in Colorado Springs and find out more about what he called 'incarnational evangelism'. I was due to travel to Colorado the month after my school's mission and I went knowing that I had given it my best shot in Oxford and it hadn't worked. Arnie took me to his local high school where I watched as he was greeted by groups of young people as we walked down the corridor. I was impressed with the warmth of relationship which he obviously had developed with them, and their obvious delight in seeing him again. All this I found very challenging, but I was able to write it off as an American thing. What changed my mind was the experience of meeting a small rock band at the school. We shared a common interest and they invited me back that evening to one of their rehearsals. Their openness was amazing and as I confidently told Arnie that this sort of thing wouldn't happen in England, a group of lads at my local school came into my mind.

During the school's mission at one of the lunch-time concerts I had been surrounded by guys who wanted to talk with me. At the time I had found comments such as, 'My brother's got a guitar' and 'I've got an amp', as slightly amusing. In the light of my experience with Arnie I realized that these comments were an attempt on the part of these guys to build a relationship with me. They wanted friendship. Unfortunately I was so intent on my own agenda that I had missed what was an open invitation to become friends.

I came back from Colorado with several pairs of Levi's and a resolve to return to the school and try and meet these young people. I went to see the music teacher at the school and I arranged to offer informal guitar lessons at lunch-times. Then I did another assembly and asked anyone who was in a band to meet me in the hall at break-time. It was a success – I had a queue of lads waiting to see me. Within a week or so I was meeting four or five groups of young people who were in bands and there were about twenty beginners happily strumming away in the music room every Thursday lunch-time. My ten years' relational youthwork at Oxford School had started. This work forms the backdrop to Chapter 3 where relational youthwork is explained as a theoretical model. Each stage in my journey is reflected in this chapter. The theory of relational outreach I present was generated by the questions raised by trying, and sometimes failing, to find a way forwards for the work with these young people.

In my first flush of enthusiasm, I have to admit that I was much too critical of the fellowship group method of youthwork. I was convinced that the relational style of work was the only answer to the immense task of reaching out to the wide diversity of young people in British society. I realize now that my critical stance to what was the majority of church-based work was very unfair and somewhat misguided. In my defence I would say that I was filled with enthusiasm for what I had found out. It has been my job with the archbishop which has given me a much broader insight into the reality of youthwork on the ground. Once again I am able to travel round the country and my eyes have been opened. I have met so many church-based youth ministers who have seen remarkable success in their work that I have been forced to revise my opinions.

The result of this rethink is presented in Chapter 1 where I spell out what I call the two disciplines of youth ministry. I now understand the importance of both the relational and the fellowship group approaches to work with young people. In a way the seeds of this perspective were there in the first mission in the schools in Oxford where the coffee bars in the other churches were self-evidently successful. Further travels in the United States and contact with Young Life, however, has convinced me of the importance of relational 'contact work' as an addition to the fellowship group style of ministry. How this could work is also spelled out in detail at the end of Chapter 1.

My journey of discovery in youth ministry has not been a solo effort. I have been extremely fortunate in working alongside a number of very skilled and insightful colleagues. The insights into relational youthwork presented in this book are very much a team effort. In 1988 Kenny Wilson from Scripture Union, Bob Dupee from Young Life in Canada, Tina Freimuth from Young Life USA and I started Oxford Youth Works. Oxford Youth Works was a course designed to train people in relational outreach. Over the years staff have come and gone, but each has contributed to our collective wisdom. I owe a good deal to these people, they are: Jude Levermore, Sam Richards, Nick Allen, Anna Chakka George, Hannah Barnes, Lyn Wyatt and Darren James.

As plans for the new training course were coming together I felt the need to return to theological study. I spent two years travelling to Birmingham University where I did an MA in Religion and Culture. The course introduced me to two areas of thinking which have together enriched my understanding of youth ministry. The first is the sociology of youth subcultures. At Birmingham I became aware of the work of the Centre for Contemporary Cultural Studies. As a youthworker I was aware of the richness of the cultural world of young people. Suddenly here was a whole body of literature which was an aid to unlocking this world and developing ideas concerning the meaning of the way young people chose to act, dress, make music, etc. The subsequent result of my investigations into questions concerning youth culture and popular culture are presented in Chapter 4 of this book.

The second area of thinking was the whole field of mission studies. While I was doing my MA, I began to realize that the insights and approaches which were developing in countries around the world could be of considerable help in my own work with young people. Although missionaries had started to develop theology in the culture and context of people in Africa, the Pacific Islands, Asia and Latin America, it was clear to me that youth culture might be a context for similar exploration. By combining the insights from the study of youth cultures with the theological methods which were now commonplace in missiology, a contextualized theology of young people might emerge. My current understanding of contextualization is presented in Chapter 5, and in Chapter 6 I develop these ideas in two short case studies to show how different styles of youth ministry might emerge from this kind of theological approach.

A contextualized theology of young people inevitably brings about changes in the Church. My own journey in respect of the relationship between young people and the Church has been affected by two very different experiences. The first came when I walked into the big top at Greenbelt and encountered the embryonic Nine O'Clock Service. I must have stayed for about ten minutes, but what I saw was enough of an inspiration to realize that contextualization of youth culture needed to be carried into the worship of the Church. This was the extent of my contact with NOS, but in Oxford I decided to work with the young people I knew to create a service which was based on their cultural expression. The result was a service which we called JOY. Being creative in worship was a real challenge and my reflections on this experience form the background to the second half of Chapter 7 on sacraments and creativity.

The second experience has come through my links with the Soul Survivor festival where I have been very happy to form part of the team during the last three years. At Soul Survivor

Introduction

I have been exposed to the growing move towards the development of 'youth churches'. I have had cause to revise my opinions once again and these are the thoughts which I present at the start of Chapter 7. Youth ministry is a growth area in the life of the Church. The current scene is characterized by considerable innovation and experimentation. Amidst all of this activity there is a need for some of us to take a few steps back from time to time and reflect on the way we are working with young people. This book represents my own thinking over the last few years. We all stand on the shoulders of those who went before us. I hope that others will read this and find it to be a helpful 'leg up' in seeking to present Christ afresh in each generation.

1

The Two Disciplines of Youth Ministry:
Outside-in or Inside-out?

CHRISTIAN YOUTHWORK CAN be divided into two quite different traditions or disciplines.[1] The first tradition is characterized by work which starts with young people who have been brought up in the Church, while the second has concentrated on ministry amongst those who are outside the Church. From the pioneer days of youthwork in the nineteenth century, these two basic approaches to Christian youthwork have been in evidence. Each generation of youthworkers has developed significant initiatives which broadly fall within these two areas. Some have focused their work on groups of Christian young people and others have concentrated on work with those who are outside the Church. The methods of youthwork developed by Christians are divided by whether the work starts outside or inside the Church. Similarly Christian youthwork organizations generally fall into one of these two traditions.

The first tradition can be called 'inside-out' because it starts with young people who are inside the Church. But one of the main aims of Christian groups formed from young people who are already believers is to attract new non-Christian members and introduce them to the faith. Thus inside-out starts with those inside who then reach out. The second tradition can be called 'outside-in', starting with those young people who are outside the Church and working to bring them in eventually. These categories are in no way meant to imply that one tradition is primarily evangelistic and the other primarily concerned with nurturing already existing faith. Neither would it be correct to say that one is concerned solely with the Church and the other with 'society' at large. Rather the distinction made between these two traditions is based upon three main factors:

i) where the work starts;
ii) the methodology adopted;
iii) assumptions about culture and faith.

This chapter sets out the case for dividing youthwork into two traditions by exploring their distinctive starting points, methodologies and assumptions. The differences between these two kinds of youthwork are then explored in greater detail. Before that, however, there are some introductory remarks that need to be made concerning the use of the terms 'youthwork' and 'youth ministry' and also the understanding of 'tradition' and 'discipline' which shape the structure of this book.

Youthwork and Youth Ministry

We are currently experiencing a resurgence of Christian work amongst young people. These are very exciting times to be involved in Christian youthwork. New initiatives and projects are springing up all around the country. Since the early 1980s more and more youthworkers are being employed by churches and Christian organizations. One result of this has been that we are seeing increased experimentation in the way that Christians work with young people.

The use of the term 'youth ministry' is linked to this new wave of full-timers. Many of us felt that our methods of working gave us a distinctive identity. In particular we were aware that professional youthworkers were those who had passed through recognized secular youth and community courses. The new developments in work amongst young people, however, were not connected with youthwork in this sense being more firmly rooted in Christian perspectives and in many cases directly funded by the Church. The term youth ministry reflects the feeling that much of what passes for youthwork in a secular setting is of a different genus to the new kinds of work being funded by the Church.

Youth ministry in this sense is an attempt to express that there is an approach to youthwork which operates within a different code to that developed within secular youthwork which is nevertheless also professional. This method of work should be called 'ministry' because its closest partner remains the clergy who also refer to their practice as ministry. Some have expressed this relationship more explicitly by adopting the title 'youth pastor'. It would be possible to speak of those who work inside-out as youth ministers and those working outside-in as Christian youthworkers. Alongside these patterns of work there may also be Christians who work within projects which follow the secular philosophy generally associated with youth and community work.

These distinctions, while containing some sense of these two terms, remain a little unsatisfactory. In the first instance youthwork' has never been solely applied to work in secular settings. Christians have also used the term for work both within the Church and work outside. For Christians youthwork has historically been a broad term covering evangelism and Christian nurture as well as the principles and values advocated by youth and community work courses. A Christian youthworker therefore might be engaged in either of these areas. In terms of the two traditions discussed in this book, it would be misleading to speak of the church-based work as youth ministry and work outside the Church as youthwork.

A further factor in the use of these terms is that many Christians feel that their work which may be 'outside the Church' has a deep spiritual significance. The ministry of the Church is seen as being to those both inside and outside the Church. Youth ministry therefore is a term which could express this fact. It is also the case that many Christians who have been trained in secular youthwork courses and employed in the statutory sector have also seen their vocation to work with young people in spiritual terms. The present interest in spiritual development as part of the youthwork curriculum signals that the labelling of the statutory sector as 'secular' is something of a misnomer.[2] There are indications that in the areas of practice and training, Christian perspectives may well find an increasing acceptance by the wider youthwork community.[3]

The confusion over terminology is a result of new developments in Christian work amongst young people. Those who wish to locate themselves firmly within the Church may well choose 'youth ministry', while those working in regular contact with Local Education Authorities (LEAs) and other agencies may well prefer 'youthwork'. My own feeling is that the use of the term youth ministry solely for work inside the Church and youthwork for work outside the Church tends to perpetuate a sacred/secular divide which I would not wish to support. My experience working with groups from the Church and with young people from outside a Christian context is that my role is to be a kind of 'amphibian' – able to exist in the water and on the land. Youthworker as 'frog' may not be an attractive proposition I realize, but the ability to change environments comfortably is a basic skill required of all youthworkers. The youthworker who is locked in a Church context is evangelistically and culturally severely limited. The youthworker only able to relate to non-Christians doesn't get a job (or if he or she does get it, conflict with the Church soon ensues). It is the ability to move successfully between the world of the Christian Church and the world of young people which characterizes successful youthwork of either tradition.

For these reasons I have decided to use youthwork and youth ministry interchangeably in this book.

Tradition and Discipline

Christian youthwork has survived by the ability to develop patterns of work and shared values. In most cases these patterns have been handed down from individual to individual within the structures provided by voluntary organizations. Tradition in this sense is well understood by those within organizations such as Crusaders, the YMCA, Scripture Union or the Boys Brigade.[4] Tradition, however, can also be used to describe the similarities which exist across organizational boundaries. The analysis of Christian youthwork in this chapter is based on dividing the majority of work on the ground into two different groups. These are hypothetical models created to give a broad understanding of what is a fairly diverse scene.

Sociologists would speak of these models as 'ideal types'. An ideal type is a theoretical construct or generalization. The generalization is used to make a clear picture from a number of complicated and seemingly different situations. An ideal type summarizes in a simplified form the basic characteristics of a way of working or behaving.[5] Each of the 'traditions' of Christian youthwork, outside-in and inside-out, is therefore an ideal type. The generalization attempts to describe how a number of separate and varied youthwork practices developed by Christians in different places and in different times might be categorized and therefore more clearly understood.

The use of generalizations or ideal types has a number of drawbacks. In the first instance the way we do youth ministry is extremely diverse and the distinctions which we understand between one way of working and another can be very subtle. To generalize about only two basic traditions may therefore be seen as reductive and inaccurate. Individual youthworkers may feel that their work moves between and beyond the descriptions offered. This may well be the case and I recognize that this sensitivity has some validity. Ideal types are not, however, designed to be a complete description of everything which is happening on the ground. The idea of two traditions is a useful tool because it offers a clarity of thought in what can at times be a fairly complex and confusing situation. The validity of the insights offered, by what I freely admit is a theoretical construct, depends upon the extent to which it sheds light on our practice as Christian youthworkers.

Linked to the idea of tradition is that of 'discipline'. It is understood that teaching is a separate profession to youthwork and therefore teachers operate within a quite different discipline from that of youthworkers. This means that it is possible to work with the same group of young people both as a youthworker and as a teacher, but to do so successfully involves the ability to switch between the two disciplines. If a teacher working in a youth club fails to change their style of relating to young people and tries to act as a teacher in this new setting, then problems begin to emerge. Young people become unresponsive to, or even resentful of, what they feel is an inappropriate discipline (I mean this in both senses of the word). For the youthworker who enters a classroom setting but who fails to adopt the discipline of teaching, different problems come to the surface. Young people in my experience tend to riot! Teachers often recognize that youthwork represents a different approach to working with young people by saying that they would not want to try to be a youthworker with young people they also teach. In other words while they might be able to switch disciplines, such a move is more problematic when dealing with the same young people. The reason why these problems arise is because teaching and youthwork are two quite different disciplines.

The recognition that teaching and youthwork represent distinctive and separate ways of working with young people is widely recognized. Indeed while it was once the case that trained teachers were also seen as being qualified as youthworkers, this is no longer the case in England. It is my argument that a similar kind of distinction needs to be brought into play between those youthworkers who work from inside the Church out to the unchurched and those who start by ministering solely amongst the unchurched and hope to see them embrace the faith. Whether such a distinction should also be institutionalized in training for youth ministry I am as yet undecided. The main purpose at this stage of arguing for such a division is to gain clarity within the present youthwork scene.

The discipline of youth ministry expressed as a set of rules can be seen in commonly held and understood social relationships. How youthworkers and young people relate to each other and behave within a practical youthwork setting is linked to these rules. The problems which youthworkers experience on a regular basis can be explained by a lack of clarity concerning the nature of the two disciplines. An example of this would be the trouble youthworkers experience when they try to connect a group of unchurched young people to a church group, or when young people from outside the Church behave inappropriately in a church service. Both of these situations can be much better understood and appropriate action taken if it is realized that work with Christian groups and work with unchurched groups are very different. The problem has come about because of a lack of clarity or because of a desire to blur the distinction between the two approaches. Youth ministry works best when we are clear in our own minds which discipline we are working within. One reason for this is that each discipline has its own internal logic. This not only dictates the structure of the work, but also applies to the way relationships are built and developed. The disciplines have slightly different approaches to working with both groups and individuals. Each discipline has different ways in which the Christian message is proclaimed, how young people are nurtured in the faith and how they then relate to the local church.

Clarity concerning the particular discipline which is in operation is essential for successful work to grow and develop. At its most basic level there needs to be a consistency in youthwork practice so that the young people involved know where they are. For the youth minister there needs to be a clarity in order that the structure and strategy of a particular project might evolve successfully. For churches or youthwork agencies there needs to be an understanding developed with the worker(s) so that expectations are realistic and accountability can be maintained. It is my belief that many of the problems experienced by young people, youth ministers and those managing youthwork projects stem from a lack of clear thinking about the tradition of youthwork and the appropriate discipline which is required for this tradition to work well.

First Discipline: Nucleus–Fringe (Inside-out)

Inside-out youthwork starts by gathering together a group of young people who are already connected to the life of the local church. Often the children of Christian parents are invited to form the basis of the group.[6] Sometimes the group will have graduated from the Sunday school classes in the church or from a confirmation group. The group may well have a title such as the 'youth group' or 'youth fellowship'. Through a combination of social activities and a programme of teaching, prayer and worship the group is encouraged and built up in the faith. In this way they form a 'nucleus' of lively Christians. The core group, however, are also encouraged to invite other

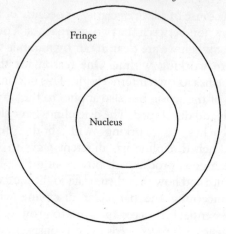

young people to join the group. Evangelism is a major priority in the group's life together.

Outreach therefore happens most effectively when these young people are in ongoing relationships with non-Christians at school or in other social activities. The network of social contact which these young people sustain is vital to the evangelistic capabilities of the youthwork. The friends of group members can be seen as another group spread around the nucleus, often referred to as the fringe of the group. A fringe member might also be someone with church connections who attends occasionally. The social activities of the group may well be organized to facilitate the natural process whereby fringe members might become part of the group.

Those who work within this tradition of youth ministry emphasize that young people are by definition in touch with youth culture. As Tricia Williams puts it, 'Teenagers may not have the maturity or depth of teaching of older Christians, but they are still the ones who are best equipped to communicate with their peers at school. They speak the language, they understand the trends in fashion and music; they share the same concerns and interests.'[7] The feeling that young people are fully involed in the teenage world has led some people to suggest that, 'The best people to reach out to young people are young people themselves.'[8]

The vast majority of Christian youthwork adopts a nucleus–fringe or inside-out approach. Church youth groups, Crusader groups and Christian Unions in schools and universities generally operate within this tradition. Most Christian outreach relies upon the basic dynamic of a Christian young person inviting someone they already know along to a meeting or an event. The pattern for town, school and university missions bears this out. Success of a mission does not really depend on the abilities of the evangelist or the team of helpers. Success invariably depends upon the active participation of young people. If they do not invite fringe people, one of two things happen: either the mission goes ahead with only Christians attending, or it attracts large numbers of unchurched young people who generally do not stay with the faith because they are not relationally linked to any of the church-based groups.

Friendship between Christian young people and non-Christians forms the basis for the majority of Christian youthwork, including most schools' work, Alpha Groups, Christian concerts, night clubs, coffee bars and alternative worship services. Some of the more recent initiatives involving worship or outreach in night clubs may well attract large numbers of unchurched young people, but long-term evangelistic success will almost certainly rely upon a committed group of Christian young people inviting unchurched young people to become more involved in the activities of their group. Having said this, adult youth ministers and volunteer youthworkers remain key in any nucleus-based work, although their role tends to be one of support, encouragement and backup to the friendship outreach of the group members.[9] Adults may well see their role as running a programme which provides the context within which young people can play this important role. In addition they will work to build relationships with new members, but this will generally be within the context of the regular activities of the group.

THE LIMITATIONS OF THE NUCLEUS–FRINGE APPROACH

The strengths of this tradition of Christian youthwork are unfortunately also its weaknesses. Christian young people are indeed connected through common educational and social activities with a potential fringe group, so friendship between young people provides the potential for sharing the gospel and attracting new members into the centre of the group's activity. Involvement with the youth group leads non-Christians gently into an encounter with Christ in a supportive environment. The problem is that the social connections of young people are nearly always limited. Most of us make friends with people who are socially very similar to ourselves. Like almost always attracts like. The nucleus–fringe tradition of youthwork is therefore limited by its starting point. If the group is formed around one type of young person, then the likelihood is that it will only attract similar young people.[10] A predominance of relatively wealthy middle-class young people in our group will lead to a middle-class group. The young people coming to faith will be 'unchurched' but they will be the unchurched of a particular type. Reliance on friendship evangelism ensures that we only reach those young people who fit the existing social make-up of the group.

There will be some young people who do not precisely fit the social mix, but invariably they will be young people who want to fit. Joining a church group may be attractive for some young people because it offers a route to move up the social scale. Those who are socially fairly distant from the regular make-up of the church tend to join in ones and twos. In later life these young people are sometimes seen as trophies by a slightly patronizing church leadership. 'That's Jim, born and brought up in the area. He's the salt of the earth,' we hear the minister say. Unfortunately for every one Jim there are probably ten or twenty other young people who have tried to find a place within the church but found the social make-up of the congregation too uncomfortable. They feel that they do not fit and so conclude that the Christian faith is not for people like them.

The nucleus–fringe approach is favoured by Christian youthworkers because it is extremely successful in socializing young people into the life of the Church. As new members join the group they are also introduced to the behaviours, beliefs, values and language of the wider Church community. In most cases church attendance is actively encouraged. The close relationship between the Church and the nucleus approach is both a strength and a weakness.

The nucleus approach is therefore limited by the extent to which the local church is able to accommodate a variety of social groups within its life and worship. A youthworker may be able to develop contact with a group of local young people who are from the neighbourhood of the church, but it is very often the case that these young people find it hard to gain acceptance by the existing church membership. In some cases disapproval of the dress and behaviour of young people may be overtly expressed by church members or by clergy.[11] If this is not the case then the language and assumptions of education and literacy which generally characterize worship simply serves to alienate the young people. In some cases they express this by disruptive behaviour, but more often they simply conclude that church is not for them.

Second Discipline: Incarnational Outreach (Outside-in)

From the earliest days Christians working with young people have recognized that they need to develop two different strategies. One for working with young people committed to the Church which attracts people in, and one which is primarily aimed at those who are socially distant from the Church. In the nineteenth century Christians talked about work which sought out the 'poor' or the 'ragged'. In more recent times we have recognized that there are particular needs amongst those 'on the frontiers' or 'secondary modern' young people, or working-class or urban and rural young people.

In every generation some Christian youthworkers have felt called to develop initiatives which are aimed at those communities and groups perceived, for whatever reason, to be distant from the make-up of the Church. Organizations such as the YMCA or Frontier Youth Trust bear witness to this calling. These organizations are part of the youthwork heritage of the Christian community, but they do not represent what we would see as the mainstream of Christian work amongst young people. The present-day Christian youthwork scene is characterized by the nucleus–fringe tradition of work and when churches talk about youthwork they almost always are talking about this tradition. The reason for this, as far as I see, is not due to a lack of social concern.

As I have said, each generation during the last 150 years has sought to share the gospel with those seen as falling outside the predominantly middle-class nature of the Church. The problem has been that in most cases these particular initiatives have seen only partial success.[12] Working outside-in is very challenging and is prone to failure. In contrast the nucleus–fringe approach in targeting one or two relatively privileged social groups has gone from strength to strength. When churches have worked only with the unchurched, their efforts often have a short life. An example of this is the way that church-based open youth clubs have declined in the last twenty years. Initiatives based on middle-class, educated groups, in contrast, have often been so successful that these youth ministries have continued to the present day, e.g. camps and house parties for public school boys and girls. While the nucleus approach may well be the main approach adopted by Christians, it is important to recognize that Christians working outside-in have been the pioneers who have in many cases developed approaches and methods of working which have been taken up by the wider youthwork world. Christian work which is funded by LEAs is based upon values and methods of work which were originally pioneered by the Church seeking to share the Christian faith and show social concern with those outside the Church. Over the last forty years, however, this work has been secularized by the youthwork profession.[13]

To work outside-in is to step outside predominantly Christian groups. It is to move youthwork beyond a church setting into the local community. Outside-in means that youthworkers aim to work with individuals, groups or communities who are socially and culturally distant from the existing Church. The youthworker moves outside the Christian group to 'be with' those who are outside the life of the Church. 'Being with' is adopted as a means of sharing the gospel. It is for this reason that many people who have explored this

12

tradition have seen their work as being 'incarnational' in nature.[14] The incarnation of Jesus is interpreted as an example of the way that those working outside-in should minister. In the life of Jesus we see God becoming a human being to build relationship with humanity. In the same way the youthworker goes to a particular group of young people to share the gospel. While the nucleus group is based upon unchurched young people joining in with the activities of the group, working outside-in requires the youthworker to partici-pate in the life of unchurched young people. The nucleus tradi-tion invites people in, the incarnational tradition goes out with the aim that young people may eventually join in the life of the Church.

'Being with' gives the relational basis from which evan-gelism might develop. Those working outside-in often speak of 'meeting young people where they are at'. This often involves focusing upon particular needs, thus the emphasis of the work may well include attention to issues such as drugs, homelessness, teenage pregnancy and alcohol. It might be that in a particular town or area young people are seen as a 'problem' by members of the Church or by the wider com-munity. Working outside-in may well come about because of the needs of adults to feel that something is being done for or about 'the kids'.

A common response of the Church to the challenge of work-ing outside-in has been to develop informal halfway houses where young people and youthworkers are able to meet. The open youth club has been the primary example of this. In the open club young people are invited to take part in activities or just to sit around. Workers will seek to build relationships with them in the context of the activities.[15] A similar plan can be seen in groups which run a drop-in centre or alcohol-free bar or advice centre. In all of these the young people remain within their own friendship groups. They are not expected to abandon their shared behaviours or values. The youth minister is seeking to meet them on their own turf. Of course the need to maintain rules and basic standards of behaviour within a club or other activity will mean that the youth minister will have to come to some agreement with the groups of young people attending.

Alongside the provision of places where encounters between youthworkers and young people can take place, this tradition of youthwork has tended in more recent times to move towards a more detached approach. In detached youth ministry a youthworker or workers will attempt to build contact with young people on the streets, in a school, or wherever groups gather together. Detached work in some Christian circles has been referred to as 'relational youthwork' with its emphasis upon relationships rather than on programmes or the provision of open clubs in buildings.

THE LIMITATIONS OF THE INCARNATIONAL APPROACH

Working outside-in is extremely demanding and difficult. To journey outside the boundaries of the Christian community to share the gospel is a tough assignment. While youthwork within the Church offers a safe and well-defined context for ministry, this may well not be the case for those working outside-in. Workers need to be those able to combine a pioneer spirit with a commitment to remain faithful to a Christian perspective. Such youthwork not only means that Christians need to go through special training, it also requires the right kind of people. To be involved, and perhaps more importantly to remain involved over the long haul, is essential. This is a matter of discernment and balance. Journeying 'outside' in order that young people might eventually find a place 'inside' not only asks a good deal of the youth minister, it also requires understanding and flexibility from those churches and Christians who support the work.

There is no doubt that young people can be very needy. Working outside-in will often involve a particular focus on young people who are in crisis or facing particular challenges. Tough problems are rarely solved overnight. Needy young people need adults who are able to offer long-term care and support. All of these issues mean that the Church may well not be able to work incarnationally/outside-in without employing the right kind of people with the right kind of skills and training.

The particular challenges which face any youth minister

working outside-in mean that effective evangelism may well be a bridge too far. Faced with the considerable problems, of first building a trusting relationship with young people outside the Church, and then meeting the challenge of the particular crises or issues with which these young people are wrestling, the worker may well feel swamped. The pain and suffering of young people can leave a youthworker feeling at a loss as to how Christ might become real in their lives.[16] This might be because problems such as homelessness, or drug abuse make the direct preaching of the gospel seem inappropriate. Young people need to be free to choose Christ for themselves, and not be manipulated or coerced into commitment when they are off-balance and vulnerable. Evangelism amongst young people who are culturally outside the Church must be contextual as well as sensitive. Many youthworkers find the challenge of expressing the faith in relevant ways to be extremely demanding. There is a tendency for proclamation of the gospel to be downplayed or ignored entirely because it is seen as being so difficult to do well. A further factor may be that Christian groups seeking money from charities or LEAs may experience pressure to adopt a less evangelistic style of work in order to receive funding. In addition to this there is the realization that even when young people do come to faith, it is thought to be very unlikely that they will be welcomed into the life of the Church.

The Dynamics of the Traditions

The distinction drawn between working inside-out and working outside-in is primarily based upon the starting point of each of the traditions. The argument that these are, in fact, two different disciplines is justified by a consideration of the internal dynamics of each of the approaches. These dynamics create fundamental differences in the two approaches. They are extremely powerful in the way that the different kinds of youthwork operate and develop and they mean that the two approaches are distinct.

THE COMMUNITY CONTEXT

The nucleus approach is intimately connected to the need for Christian parents to feel that their young people are 'safe'. In *Growing up Evangelical* I have argued at some length that the function of evangelical youthwork is to provide a safe place where Christian young people can socialize.[17] This relationship between youthwork and the needs and desires of Christian parents forms a strong undercurrent in all the activities, values and Christian teaching delivered within a church-related group. In all negotiations with the clergy or with a local church, the youthworker is working within the basic emotional dynamic which is created by the parental duties, needs and concerns of church members. This dynamic is extremely powerful and its influence cannot be underestimated. How evangelism takes place, how young people are nurtured within the faith, and how the group relates to the Church, will be determined by communication between the clergy, the youthworker, young people and Christian parents. In the majority of cases the parents, supported by the clergy, will form the most influential lobby pressurizing the youthworker and the young people. This pressure is commonly felt when working inside-out.

When we move into the wider community and work outside-in, we find that not only the method of working has to change. More importantly the pressure which comes from the quite justified concerns of Christian parents does not form any part of the atmosphere within which the work progresses. Clergy and parents are not on the sidelines approving or disapproving of what is going on. The youth minister is therefore not subject to influence and lobbying which can very often form part of the church scene. When we work incarnationally amongst a group of young people the key dynamic which operates will be the relationship between the gospel commitments of the worker and the already existing values of the local community. Parents of young people and the wider community will judge the appropriateness of the work according to their own moral framework. The task of the youth minister is to work contextually, to start by valuing the already existing morality and values of the community within which he or she is working. In any community there will be ways of behaving and relating which are not only seen as 'right', they might also be regarded by the Christian as a vestige or reflection of the kingdom of God. To work outside-in is to start by affirming the positive in a particular community. To fail to do so will mean that the wider community of parents and neighbours and community leaders will see the work as an alien intrusion and 'out of order'.

ASSUMING A SUBCULTURE

The nucleus approach assumes the subculture of the Church to be the appropriate medium for evangelism and Christian worship. To join a nucleus group is to participate in a process of socialization into an already existing church subculture. This subculture is characterized by a common set of behaviours, language, values and perspectives. Within the subculture of the Church it may well be the case that the youth ministry will be innovative or even seen as on the edge in one way or another. This does not mean that the youth ministry has moved from one subculture to another. In most cases youth ministry which is pioneering will be the means by which the church subculture renews itself. Church young people grow up to become key members of local churches. The youth leaders of today will often be the church leaders of tomorrow. These leaders take with them the insights and methods of working which they adopted in their youth ministry. In this way the youth ministry of fifteen years ago has become the mainstream of church life today. One of the places where this is most obvious is the change in music used in church services. Most evangelical churches now have some kind of guitar-based music group leading worship. This practice has its roots in the youthwork of the 1960s and 1970s.

The nucleus discipline therefore works within an already contextualized expression of the faith. The church subculture is a cultural construction which connects the values of the gospel with a particular social context. To argue that church subculture is one possible expression of the Christian faith in our context is not the same as saying that this subculture is 'wrong'. It is simply to say that outside the subcultural context of the Church, this expression of the faith needs to be re-evaluated. Working incarnationally as opposed to the nucleus approach does not assume the subculture of the Church to be normative. To work outside-in is to seek to see the gospel contextualized amongst a group of people who were not previously part of the Church. The hope is that Jesus can become real within the subculture which these people share. To say this is not to baptize a particular subculture uncritically. The gospel will act redemptively to bring about the values and behaviours which are characteristic of the kingdom of God. Redemption will involve an affirmation of some aspects of subcultural life and a critique of others. The priority will be that the youth ministry will not seek to impose an expression of the faith which has evolved in one particular social context. The aim throughout will be to see people begin to live out the Christian faith with integrity and faithfulness within their own community context.

For the youthworker this process involves a journey of discovery. In the first place there is a need to set aside the security which the certainties of church work offer. Within a missiological context Charles Kraft has used the language of 'paradigm shift' to describe the movement of the gospel and the missionary from one cultural context to another.[18] This shift does not deny the validity of what a church context has taught us, it just recognizes that true engagement with different cultures and subcultures raises different questions of the Christian faith and the Bible. From these questions emerges an interpretation of the faith which should remain true to the gospel and yet nuanced in a way which is fresh and distinctive.

The Rules of the Disciplines

The nucleus approach operates within a set of clearly defined rules. How young people are expected to behave in their personal lives and in the life of the group is closely defined. Issues to do with sex, drugs, alcohol, swearing, smoking, etc. will be discussed frequently and expectations will be made very clear. When the rules of the group are breached in some way the leaders will take steps to try and normalize the situation.

The strict adherence to behavioural codes arises from the well-defined standards expected by Christian parents and the Church. When youthworkers allow groups to step beyond these rules serious problems start to emerge. If for instance a youth group is found to be involved in any way with drug-taking, the youthworker can expect to be relieved of his or her position. Christian young people and parents expect, and most probably need, a fairly well-defined setting within which to explore the Christian faith. When youthworkers allow a freer interpretation of the rules, it is not unusual for Christian young people to go a little over the top. The youth group party where young people get desperately drunk would be a good example of this kind of problem. A clear set of boundaries and rules are essential to the successful working of a nucleus group. They form a part of the package and while they may be renegotiated a little, they are properly part of the scenery. In contrast when youthworkers work outside-in a much more complicated picture begins to emerge.

To work incarnationally is to start by accepting young people as they are. The youthworker first needs to build a non-judgemental relationship which means understanding comes before setting down rules. A youthworker may well be witness to and aware of behaviour which is not only well out of court for the church youth group, but may also be illegal. The worker may well conclude that some of what passes for normal behaviour in the group, such as racist comments, is completely out of step with the gospel. How this perspective may be shared involves a negotiation between worker and young people. The worker will need to make a decision as to the extent to which he lets such things pass because he wishes to remain in relationship with the group or individual. Along-side this the worker will need to balance the extent to which his presence, or his silence, compromises his integrity as a Christian youth minister. Such a dilemma does not occur in working in a nucleus group – or at least it shouldn't! – while it is the everyday stuff of working outside-in.

The manner of the youth minister who engages with a group incarnationally will need to be primarily that of a learner. The behaviour of the group may well jar with the values of the worker at first, but the aim is to move beyond this to find the underlying values of the group. The good which is there in every subculture could take a little time to become evident and the worker needs to gain understanding. It is only out of a sympathetic knowledge of both the good and the bad that the worker can present Jesus as someone who can meet the group within their own cultural world. The aim is that behaviour and values emerge from a transformational encounter between Jesus and the group. The hope is that as this begins to happen, the group become distinctively followers of Jesus within their own subcultural context. To help this happen, the worker needs to effect a change from someone who is building relationships and understanding to someone who is a leader within that group context. The ability to effect this change in relationship from participant observer to one who is seeking to bring about change and renewal, is fundamental to success in incarnational ministry. This aspect of working incarnationally is qualitatively different from the discipline of work in a church context.

CHURCH

The nucleus group is generally rooted in a church setting. The young people who make up the core of the group will often come from church-going, committed families. Most groups are formally linked to one particular church. While the church may well see the need for separate activities, and even different worship services for the young people, the links will, in most cases, remain strong. The young people of the church are rightly seen as a vital part of the whole community of the church body. Theologically and practically this means that young people in a nucleus group really cannot be talked about as if they are a separate church. They form a part of the wider Christian community however their meetings are organized. Having said this, the reality is that young people meeting together are part of the Church. When young people form church families and their friends start to experiment with worship, it is important that ways are found to express the genuine 'churchness' of what they are doing.[19]

When working outside-in the relationship between this new

group of Christian young people and the Church is a little less clear. To see the gospel contextualized in a cultural setting which is distinct from the existing local church may well mean that what is appropriate would be something more akin to a new church plant. The eventual aim of the work would be the establishment of a new church which reaches out to people of all ages within that particular subculture. This new church will need to come to some resolution with the wider Church community. My own feeling is that such initiatives need the tradition, stability and support of existing denominations or church groups to avoid going down the route of narrow and authoritarian sectarianism. To church plant in this manner involves very different skills and structures from work in a nucleus or church setting.

Mixing up the Disciplines

The argument for dividing Christian youthwork into two separate but complementary disciplines is primarily based on the need for clarity. It is fundamental to my argument that both of these traditions of youthwork have a place in the life of the Church. The nucleus model has come about because the Church has a duty to bring up its own young people in the faith. This approach is rightly evangelistic. Indeed Bob Clucas argues that without the steady involvement of non-Christian young people in youth groups and Christian camps and house parties the nucleus model simply doesn't work. Clucas argues, and I think rightly, that Christian young people need to feel that the faith has the power to change people.[20] They are themselves built up in the faith by seeing their friends come to faith. A nucleus group which does not have a regular injection of new enthusiasm and members tends to stagnate.

However, the Church also has a duty to try and share the gospel message with the wider community. Every church should seek to encourage its own teenagers to remain a part of the Church, but it is probably not the case that every church should engage in working outside-in. This is partly a matter of resources. To engage incarnationally with communities distant from the Church is costly and involves particular skills and resources. It is therefore probably more realistic to expect groups of churches in an area to supplement the nucleus model by joining together to support a more experimental model of incarnational outreach. In some cases this is best done through setting up an independent charitable group dedicated to this kind of work, or by forming a partnership with an existing parachurch group such as Youth For Christ, Crusaders or Scripture Union. Churches will always be inclined to look to helping their own young people before they engage in mission amongst other groups, this I feel is very proper. However, there probably needs to be a decision to tithe to support outside-in work. One approach might be for churches in an area who are appointing youthworkers to join together and agree that at least one of the posts should focus upon groups of young people who are unlikely to be touched by the nucleus approach.

Work which is outside-in is vulnerable to subversion by the Church. Most churches are committed to outreach, but they habitually see this in terms of the inside-out model of ministry. When outside-in work begins to get going, the habitual values and behaviours of the Church seem to gently take the power and energy out of the ministry. This will never be a deliberate policy, it simply emerges when the two disciplines are confused or when attempts are made to merge the two approaches, such as when involvement in the existing youth group or church is seen as the next step for young people who have come to faith through incarnational outreach in the local community. This strategy may work occasionally, but more often than not enthusiastic and articulate local young people have the energy sapped from them because they are introduced to the more developed and authoritative subculture of the church group. Suddenly the lively and original ways in which they first spoke of their new Christian experience are replaced by the standardized jargon of the Church. In some cases these new young people simply fade from the Christian scene. If they remain involved with the Church, they tend to become disconnected from their home culture and communities by the socializing nature of the Christian group. In the church group they become more Christian, but they can also become more middle-class.

The subversion of outside-in work can also come about when youthworkers themselves blur the boundaries. One example of this I know of involved a group of unchurched young people who came to faith through outreach on the streets. The worker realized that a separate worship service which emerged from their culture would probably be the best next step. Soon a lively worship service got underway using dance music and visuals as well as a commitment to charismatic ministry. Local church groups soon got to hear of this event and they started to come along. Soon an event which was based on fifty or so unchurched young people had grown to become a mixed group of 400 churched and unchurched. The success of the service was amazing and the worker and his team were very excited. The problem was that within a year every one of the unchurched young people had disappeared from the service. None of them made a fuss, they seemed to go very quietly. In fact they went so quietly that the youthworker didn't even notice. The departure of the original group was disguised by the roller-coaster success of the service.

Blurring the boundaries often comes about when churches are appointing full-time youthworkers. The job descriptions of church youthworkers are a horror genre all of their own. Chief amongst these horrors, in my view, is the inability of committees and clergy to resolve the problem of which discipline of youth ministry they expect to see happening on their patch. There is an idealism which sets in and expects both approaches of the same person. Most of us have a commitment to both work with young people in the Church and to reach out to those who will not join our church groups. Unfortunately, in my experience, very few of us are able to sustain active and lively ministry in both of these areas at the same time. The reality is that we either favour one or the other. Over time problems set in. If we favour outside-in over inside-out work, we may end up losing our job because Christian parents and clergy perceive us as failing. If we favour inside-out work over outside-in, then we may keep the Church happy but we may not achieve all we hope for in our outreach work.

At heart these problems arise from a misunderstanding of the importance of both disciplines of youth ministry. In many people's minds evangelism to the unchurched inevitably means some kind of outside-in model of ministry. The church youth group reaching out to a fringe is not valued highly enough as a method of outreach.[21] In other situations this confusion is reversed and the nucleus group is seen as the only successful Christian approach to youthwork and incarnational ministry is rejected because it is not based in the Church or because it is seen as a watering down of the gospel. The future of youth ministry in the Church may well only be secured if we are able to articulate the difference between these two disciplines of youth ministry. Youthworkers themselves need to be clear what they are setting out to do and present their work honestly to the Church as being either one or the other kind of approach. Training for youthwork needs also to embrace these distinctions and train people appropriately for their particular calling. In addition to this, those in the Church making decisions about the direction of youthwork and the allocation of resources need to adopt this two-disciplined framework in order that young people of all kinds have the gospel shared with them in the way which is most appropriate to their particular culture.

2

A Theology of Youth Ministry

THERE IS A difference between a theology of youth ministry
and a theology of young people. It is when groups of young
people begin to speak of their encounter with God that a
theology which is indigenous to them begins to emerge. A
theology of youth ministry, on the other hand, seeks to demon-
strate how our understanding of God shapes and influences
the practice of youth ministry. This chapter is an attempt to
link what we believe as Christians – our theology – to what
we do as youthworkers.

Youth Ministry and the Mission of God

We work amongst young people because of the God we
believe in. The Bible speaks of a God who crosses boundaries
to build relationships with people. This is the God of
Abraham, Isaac, Jacob and Moses. We meet him in the burning
bush, the still small voice, the vision in the temple and walking
in the garden with Adam. This is the God whom we see assum-
ing human form in the birth of Jesus. God takes the limitations
of our own nature upon himself in order that we might experience his presence and love. At a wedding, sitting at a table, in
stories and through works of power, we see God in Jesus walking beside his disciples. Ultimately this journey leads him to
death on the cross and his triumphant resurrection. At Pentecost the resurrected presence of God falls upon his followers.
In community life, evangelism and mission, through persecu-
tion, failure, loss and suffering, the Spirit of God embraces his
people. Walking the way of Jesus becomes a Spirit-filled life
of faith.

The Christian gospel tells the story of a missionary God.[1]
Relationship is at the centre of the being of God whom we

know as Father, Son and Holy Spirit – Creator, Redeemer and
Sustainer. We see the God who is three and who is one as he
is revealed in mission. We know of God in no other way than
as one who seeks humanity in relationship. It is this God who
calls us and inspires us to reach out to young people. Youth
ministry or Christian youthwork is therefore grounded in the
missionary nature of God. The mission is God's, not ours.
We are called and inspired by God to participate in his seeking
of relationship with all human beings. Our practice as
youthworkers finds its true rationale in the God who calls us
to share in his seeking of young people.

The Practice of the Mission of God

God seeks humanity because of a radical breakdown in relationship. People are created in the image of God. We bear the
mark of the Creator. Male and female we reflect his face and
resonate to his voice. Our highest ideals and deepest desires
rest on this foundation. We are who we are because of our
createdness. But the biblical story pivots on the failure of
humanity to respond to the voice of God. We are fallen, in
rebellion and in denial. Distant from a God who calls us without being heard. We are sought by a God who desires us and
loves us. It is out of his love that he calls us to turn and meet
his embrace.

   To be truly Christian, youthwork must carry within it the
essential dynamic of the gospel story. We are called to proclaim
this gospel in both our words and deeds in ways that young
people can understand. The gospel story is rooted in a God
who is the same yesterday, today and forever. This unchanging
story, however, must be proclaimed afresh in each generation.
Our task is to seek a location within the mind-set and subculture of particular groups of young people where this story
can come to life. The gospel is thus to be 'incarnated' in the
basic expressions, lifestyle and accent of young people where
it can bless, redeem and transform individuals and communities. For some young people, the seeking God is first
encountered in the care and concern offered by youthworkers
and the Church community. The care we offer in the day-to-

26

day activities of youthwork acts as a concrete prophetic sign of the God who desires relationship, but the gospel so lived out should also be spoken. We are called to tell the story of a God who seeks relationship, a God who calls young people to worship and service in his name. With some groups of young people the telling of the story will be the starting point of youthwork. The telling of the story, however, is then reinforced by the faithful lifestyles of youth ministers who act as mentors and models on the path of discipleship.

Youth ministry is shaped by our experience of the God who calls us to mission. We do youthwork as Christians for no other reason than that we tell the gospel story. We may wish to frame our practice in terms of educational theory, counselling, community work, sport and leisure provision, or any number of other theoretical models of working with young people, but to do so as Christian youthworkers is to seek to integrate these perspectives into the overarching nature of the larger gospel story. It is this commitment to the role of the gospel as the story within which our other commitments are understood and have meaning that brings an identity to the Christian youthworker or minister. When the relationship between the gospel and other theories of working with young people is reversed the youthworker ceases to be a Christian youthworker and becomes a youthworker or community worker who happens to be Christian. For youthworkers involved in projects outside a specifically Christian setting or funded by local authorities, such a self-understanding and identity may be a matter of course.

The Shape of the Gospel

A theology of youth ministry must seek to be a distinctive expression of the gospel in the light of current social situations. The gospel story is characterized by polarities of emphasis which shape our practice. A distinctive, contextualized theology of youth ministry will depend upon how we position ourselves in relation to: the incarnation and death of Christ, the redemption of the world and repentance, the transcendence and immanence of God, the hope of his kingdom and the work of the Spirit amongst his people.

THE INCARNATION AND THE CROSS

In the story of Jesus we see life and death, joy and suffering. To emphasize the incarnation of God as a human being is to affirm social life, the physical body and human culture. The Jesus of the Gospels is sociable. In Jesus we see someone who enjoys company, who is a guest at dinner parties and present at weddings. John the Baptist is cast as the ascetic who rants in the desert, yet Jesus is accused of being a wine bibber and a friend of sinners. Jesus valued friendship highly: with Martha, Mary and Lazarus we see a deep, affectionate relationship emerge. Their grief becomes his own and forms the backdrop to the miracle of resurrection. The Jesus of the Gospels is physical: he sleeps, eats, drinks; he gets tired, needs to rest and finds the crowds a strain. In his resurrected glory he is still corporeal. 'Put your hand in my side,' he says to Thomas.[2] Children sit on his knee and the sick are healed by the touch of his hands. The incarnation locates the revelation of God in a specific time, place and culture. Jesus was a Jew with a family, a tribe, a history and an occupation. He spoke Aramaic and he knew the Hebrew scriptures, he was circumcised and an active participant in synagogue and temple worship.

When we turn to contemplate the cross of Christ, we are confronted with self-denial and suffering. At Gethsemane Jesus is tormented with the prospect of what is ahead. Betrayed, abandoned, mocked and scorned, Jesus is eventually hung up like a piece of meat and left to die. But the torment of the cross is perhaps only partially physical: 'My God, my God, why hast thou forsaken me?' tells of a deeper anguish (Mark 15.34). It is the Father who wills it and the Spirit who carries the power of it into the present, but this resolution of the Godhead leads down the path of a cosmic suffering. In an act of self-commitment to humanity and relationship, the divine Trinity tears itself apart.[3] The way of mission inevitably leads to the cross; Jesus makes this very clear. To follow him is to embrace self-denial.

28

> If any man would come after me, let him deny himself and take up his cross and follow me. For whoever would save his life, will lose it; and whoever loses his life for my sake and the gospel's will save it. (Mark 8.34–5)

The incarnation and the cross of Christ are, of course, intimately connected in the gospel story. Yet in developing a theology of youth ministry, these aspects of the story are experienced as contrasting points of attraction. Ministry which affirms life, has to be balanced with self-sacrifice and asceticism. The joy of physicality and culture and creativity is to be tempered by a sense of discipline and the higher calling of commitment to God's work. Yet at the same time, sensible, measured and temperate ministry is possibly not what is required. We are called to live lives of creative integrity. A prophetic witness in any culture will not be moderate, it will have to form itself around one of these polarities. Some will be called to the cross, while others will seek to affirm life and engage in cultural creativity. The aesthetic and ascetic, the incarnation and the cross, will coexist in the Church. Yet in each case the one will always need the other. Those walking the way of the cross must always affirm the positive nature of human life. Those who are deeply incarnated in human life and society will at one time or another be called to self-denial and suffering.

Youthwork which is incarnational will see in the life of Jesus a model for ministry. It is essential, not only to good practice, but also to the proclamation of the gospel, that relationships are at the heart of the work. Dean Borgman says that we are called to 'waste time' with young people 'hanging out' with them.[4] Unprogrammed social time will form the heart of our ministry as it seems to have done in the life of Jesus. Young people will learn to become Christian because they are in regular informal contact with Christian people who model the faith. The dilemmas and challenges of Christian discipleship will be dealt with as we are on the move from one informal activity to another – car journeys, conversations while going fishing, coffee in the kitchen, a post card sent from a trip abroad. The substance of incarnational ministry is the valuing of contact between adults and young people in the everyday and ordinary things of life. Friendship and relationship will not only be the means of ministry, they will be the ministry itself.

Youthwork which is incarnational must affirm the physicalness of life. Growth in body and mind characterize adolescence. Sex and sexuality are the key issues which young people are faced with in the teenage years. Christian youthwork cannot afford to locate itself in the midst of adolescence without a creative contribution to the storm which surrounds sexual identity and sexual behaviour. Unfortunately we inherit a Christian tradition which has seen in the cross of Christ a reason to chastise the flesh, deny passion, and ignore the body. Our bodies may well be seen as temples of the Holy Spirit, but the emphasis has tended to rest more heavily on Spirit than body. The incarnation indicates the sacredness of the physical body as a vessel worthy of God's indwelling. Youth culture celebrates the body and the Christian faith incarnated amongst young people must find appropriate ways to affirm this. Youth ministry contextualized in youth culture will see physicality and image transformed in God's sight. Our worship and our expression of fellowship must be both 'carnal' and holy. We need to affirm the image of God not as a disconnected 'Spirit' within young people, but as a renewed vision of the way that God sees us. At the same time in a culture where style and image are the highest ideal, the cross of Christ may act as a rebuke. We can sell out to relevance, we can drown our faith in culture. The cross of Jesus calls us to prize costly relationship above product. Being on the cutting edge of youth ministry means that you bleed for others, not for art.

REDEMPTION AND REPENTANCE

The gospel story pivots on the significance of the cross. The cross reveals the hidden passion of God for humanity. Father, Son and Holy Spirit break their own fellowship to restore fellowship with humanity. The cross is a cosmic enacting of the desire God has for renewed relationship with his creation. A theology of salvation which makes sense of the cross is not an optional extra for Christian youthworkers. The centrality of the death of Christ for the gospel story means that this event must be right at the heart of our practice. Faith in the saving death of Christ is not a personal conviction or peculiar evangelical bent. The death of God the Son for us must make a difference in the way we relate to young people. If we do not see how the cross might be of central significance in our work, then we are probably less than we should be as Christian youthworkers. The themes of redemption and repentance act as bridges between the lives of young people and the centre-piece of the Christian story.

The cross is central to the New Testament. There are a number of metaphors, however, which are used to tell the signifi-cance of the event.[5] The idea of redemption or ransom is one of these. Rather than a full-blown explanatory theory of how the death of Christ brings about salvation, the word 'redemp-tion' offers a snapshot or word picture of the significance of the cross. The New Testament picture of redemption is drawn from the world of the market-place and commerce. In this environment someone or something is 'redeemed' when it has been bought back.[6] The image may well be of a slave who is bought back and then set free: 'In him we have redemp-tion through his blood, the forgiveness of our trespasses, according to the riches of his grace' (Ephesians 1.7).

As the Anglican liturgy puts it, 'He opened wide his arms for us on the cross; he put an end to death by dying for us.'[7] The love of God seen in the death of Christ invites a response. Though once far off and neglectful of a relationship with the divine, we are called by the passion of God to respond. We are facing away but we turn to be greeted by our Maker. From a journey of independence and rebellion we retrace our steps and meet the love of God face on at the foot of the cross. It is the essence of the gospel story that Christ's death effects a change in people: 'When I survey the wondrous cross on which the King of Glory died, my richest gain I count but loss and pour contempt on all my pride.'[8] We are the returning son of the parable finding in our desperation a father who has waited day after day at the end of the drive to embrace us and take us home (Luke 15.11ff).

Redemption and repentance signify the dynamic of the narrative flow of the Christian story. Repentance brings a reso-lution where the estranged actors in the story eventually meet.

The loving self-giving on the part of God is completed by its acknowledgement by humanity. Love is returned with love in relationship. But to turn away from the outpouring of divine passion leads to isolation and death. Christian youthwork will locate itself within this dynamic of redemption and repentance. Every young person will be seen as being of infinite worth because of the price that has been paid for their freedom in the death of Christ. The self-worth and identity which young people are seeking to achieve will be respected but interpreted within the context of the overarching story of the gospel. Without returning to God life remains hollow however creative, energetic and positive it may be. God's passionate desire for relationship with every young person is the foundation stone of our ministry.

At the same time Christian youthworkers are called to respect and support young people whatever their response to the death of Christ. To do so is a sign of God's grace – Christ died for all and loves all. The Christian message is one of grace, before we respond. The dynamic of the gospel story has space within it for people to turn away from the passion of God. Youthwork should be characterized by a realistic and sympathetic understanding that this is the case. While repentance will form part of our desire for all people, the reality will be that some choose to remain distant from their Creator. This choice must be respected.

Turning towards the light involves a turning away from darkness. In young people's lives that which binds them and holds them down may be drug abuse, social disadvantage, poverty, bullying, or any number of implacable problems. Christian youthwork will attempt to bring liberation and empowerment in these situations by offering counsel, support and friendship. The day-to-day practical offer of care will be seen as a prophetic sign of redemption and repentance. When individual young people begin to turn and address their problems, when they cease to be victims and start to build lives full of self-confidence and creativity, the youthworker will understand her practice as the in-breaking of the kingdom of God. The young people may or may not acknowledge the divine drama which is being played out in their lives, but the youthworker will see her own work as an invitation for young people to respond to a God who continues to bleed for them, who waits for them and longs for them to come home.

Repentance will impact every aspect of a young person's life. To turn to follow Christ is to set new priorities. When we see ourselves in the face of Christ on the cross, the story of God becomes our story and life can never be the same. Our identity becomes transformed in a loving encounter with God. A change of identity is not to be confused with a change in social life or cultural appreciation. Coming to faith should not require that we substitute our culture for another culture, or our social relationships for another set of relationships. The Holy Spirit changes us to be more fully who we should be within the setting where we most naturally fit. But when we turn to God some of our behaviours, attitudes and values will become uncomfortable. We will begin to see the world through God's eyes. His concerns will become our concerns. The gospel demands that people change. An encounter with God brings renewal and challenge. Youth ministry without repentance is youth ministry without God. This is not to say that we should necessarily expect young people who turn to Christ to readily fit the culturally conditioned mores of the Church. The practical implications of repentance will be played out within each subculture as the Holy Spirit leads young people in the way of Christ. We should expect repentance and change, but youth ministers may not be able to predict what this will look like from outside a close involvement with a particular group of young people.

TRANSCENDENCE AND IMMANENCE

The Christian story tells of an unknowable God who makes himself known. We do not know God in the same way that we know about a part of his creation. We cannot make God the object of our study and enquiry. We know God as he chooses to come to us. We know God as we are caught up in his knowing of us. This aspect of Christian spirituality and experience means that faith is always mystery and never certainty. It is the moment when we think that we have got God sussed that we have actually lost sight of him.[9]

Encounter with God is dangerous. The beginning of wisdom is the fear of God. God is not a casual acquaintance or a cuddly toy. The Creator of the world is not at our beck and call. We cannot summon God up in prayer or in worship. We encounter God because he chooses to meet with us. We give ourselves to God, we do not strike up a contract. We never meet God as equals. We do not possess or own the gospel story of which we are a part. We participate in the story as players and actors keeping in step with a God who knows the next scene. Worship is the act of acknowledging the 'godness' of God and the creatureliness of humanity.

It is in the life of Christ that God is made most fully known. Faith therefore rests upon the revelation of God in Christ. We are able to encounter God in his revelation through the words of the Old and New Testaments. Our understanding of God therefore rests upon, and is judged by the revelation of God contained within the Bible. All theology is an abstraction from the authoritative biblical material. All theology, however biblical, stands outside the gospel story and is provisional, only partially or temporarily true. All our pictures of God, our habitual turns of phrase, our cherished lines from choruses teeter on the brink of idolatry, because to reduce God to our knowledge of him is to make of our theology an idol.[10]

The God of the gospel story is beyond knowing, transcendent. He is the Creator, the Alpha and the Omega. He offers himself for our contemplation in the life, death, resurrection and ascension of Christ. He meets us in a narrative, and true knowing can only be found in participation in the story. Our reflection on the biblical story is an act of faithful engagement. A search for meaning. To make our theology into a search for objective truth is to move beyond the dynamic of faith.

Youth ministry is worked out within the context of the transcendence and immanence of God. The youth minister will always be caught between the familiarity and the mystery of God. On the one hand, there is a desire to invite young people to seek a God who can be known. On the other, there should be a realization that all our knowing is to be treated carefully as an act of grace rather than a possession. The God we meet as friend and guide is also the God who is beyond comprehension and profoundly unknowable. We desperately want young people to have a meaningful faith, but we need to offer this possibility in a way which avoids idolatry. It is God who encounters young people in the midst of our programmes, relationships and spiritual activities. Our skill as youthworkers is empty without the work of the Holy Spirit. We will be tempted to guarantee encounter with God, but this we must resist. We will inevitably at times be drawn into an overreliance on techniques. In our desire for success we will turn to the latest relevant approach to evangelism. In themselves these may be of considerable worth, but their rhetoric may fool us into seeing their application as essential or inevitable. It is God who seeks young people and chooses to call them to himself. Encounter with God is a spiritual event shrouded with mystery. Despite all our efforts, training and experience, we are powerless beside the sovereign work of God.

The search for an expression of the faith which makes sense to young people is basic to Christian youthwork. The desire to communicate carries with it the possibility of simplification. Adolescence can be a time where the world is painted in very strong colours; the subtleties of shade and hue are generally a characteristic of later life. Youth ministry has, at times, served young people ill by portraying faith as clear-cut and matter-of-fact. The widespread absence of formal theological training for youth ministry means that Christian youthworkers are prone to the latest catchy trends. This has meant that the immanence of God has been emphasized at the expense of his transcendence. The otherness of a God who is to be feared and respected has often been played down. The mystery of faith has been debunked, unpacked, demythologized and illustrated into non-existence. The Creator God who comes to judge the world, in our hands has become a friend who is always by our side. Prayer is calling up God on the phone and worship is a rave in the nave. Not that in themselves any of these expressions of the faith are wrong or mistaken, God is indeed a friend, prayer can be a time of 'calling God up' and worship can be a 'rave'. It is the reduction of faith to these things and these things alone which needs to be questioned. When our simplifications leave young people with only part of the picture, is it any wonder that in later life they search for a more satisfying truth than that which they have found within the evangelical constituency?[11]

The kingdom of God was central to the teaching of Jesus. He enters onto the scene in Mark's Gospel proclaiming that the kingdom is at hand 'repent, and believe in the gospel' (Mark 1.15). The kingdom of God is ushered in with the presence of the incarnated Son of God. To be in the company of Jesus is to be close to the kingdom of God.[12] At the same time the kingdom is to be expected. We wait for the kingdom and pray for its fulfilment. The kingdom is about the end-times. These end-times are present in the life and death of Christ, but they are summed up in the eventual close of the age.

For the Christian the kingdom of God is about personal and community renewal in the present, but it is also about the assurance that God will put things to rights in the future. Christian hope therefore is concerned with an encounter with a liberating God who sets us free to see our present lives with new eyes and the future with expectation. The kingdom is about setting the prisoners free, preaching good news to the poor and giving the blind sight. Hope is in the air, and the possibility of transformed lives is brought into reality by the death and resurrection of Christ. Repentance is turning to greet these promises as a reality which is both in the present and which will eventually be fulfilled in the future.

Christian youthworkers are called to be heralds of this kingdom. Our feet are blessed as we carry good news to those we meet. We are torch bearers charged with keeping our lights shining so that others may see. Spirituality is the basic ingredient of our work, whatever discipline of youth ministry we practise. Our prayer and reflection upon the Bible and daily life is in no way marginal to our effectiveness as youthworkers. It is the expected and fulfilled hope of the kingdom which gives us the energy to interact with young people and community groups. The kingdom of God is a vision which we see in outline in the changed lives, expectations and choices which emerge in young people's lives through our work. The kingdom is what keeps us in the action as we wait expectantly for what God has promised to bring about.

To be a Christian youthworker is therefore to be a worker for the kingdom of God. The concerns of the kingdom are to become our concerns. Social inequality, economic hardship, racial prejudice, sexual discrimination, physical disability, emotional upset, educational disadvantage rightly fall within our remit. These issues are spiritual issues in that they are an offence to the kingdom of God. The secular youth service may share some of these concerns, but their agenda is not synonymous with ours. The Christian youthworker is a servant of the kingdom of God rather than a particular political or social agenda. To the extent that the desire of God for justice and equality coincides with the programmes of secular youthwork we are in accord, but this is not to say that Christian youthwork is no more than a theologically informed and understood framework. It is the message of the kingdom, not the demands of secular philosophy, which reminds us that God is concerned with the whole of life.

The Christian youthworker looks back to the cross of Christ, engages in the mission of God in the present, and looks for liberation in the future. The dynamic of the now but not yet kingdom determines our practice as youthworkers. Our ministry is shaped by the need for a vision of hope amongst young people. Hope which rests on what God has done in Christ, what he is doing in the present and what he will do at the end of the age. This is kingdom hope and it is expressed better than I am able by a meditation on hope which was written for a JOY service in Oxford.

Some people say, 'Life is a circle –
you're born, you grow up, you work,
you grow old, you die.'

Some people say, 'What will be, will be.'

Some people say, 'There are no jobs
so no one will want me.'
Some people say, 'There will always

be war – what can I do about it?'
Some people say, 'There will always be homelessness – tis a
shame.'
Some people say, 'The world's a terrible place
and I want no part in it.'
Some people say, 'Who knows what my life will be like
tomorrow, I'll just wait and see.'

Hope says, 'Bollocks'.

Hope helps you see a different reality,
a world where anything is possible
not just for tomorrow but for today.

Hope helps you see, not just what things could be like
but what today is like
in a different light.

Hope is not an empty promise
or a dream of escaping.

Hope changes the colour of
the world we live in.

Hope changes our faces from
the faces of the bored and the defeated
to the faces of those who
see life as an adventure.

Life requires risk, experiment,
adventure, possibility.
In short life requires hope.

If there's no hope, there's no point.
With God there's never no point. [13]

THE HOLY SPIRIT AND HUMAN ACTIVITY

The Holy Spirit is an active partner with the Father and the Son
in every part of the gospel story. The Spirit is there moving
across the primal waters, it is by means of the Spirit that the
stuff of life is changed and brought into being. As the Spirit
descends upon Jesus at his baptism we are given a privileged
glimpse into the creative energy of communication which

flows between the Father and the Son. The life of Jesus is one
which is worked out in fellowship and with the energy and
activity of the Holy Spirit. At Pentecost the Holy Spirit descends upon the disciples in tongues of fire. They begin to
speak in languages other than their own and as they preach
the gospel works of wonder and the Spirit's power characterize
their witness. God is three and God is also one. The Holy Spirit
does not just appear at the end of the story to bless the Church.
The Holy Spirit, with the Father and the Son plays a fully
scripted role in every aspect of the story.

The advent of the charismatic movement and recent new
waves of God's blessing have tended to confuse the youthwork
situation. There are many points of difference between
Christian churches concerning the action of the Holy Spirit.
My own view is that these differences are something to be cele-
brated and enjoyed. It is the distinctive elements in spirituality
and Christian worship which tend to hold my fascination.
Those things which we hold in common, are extremely important, but when worship and spiritual life is reduced to these
things alone the result tends to leave me a little cold. A theology
of youth ministry needs to draw upon the breadth of our
present understanding of God. At the same time we need to
be critical of our ecclesiastical, tribal affiliations, especially
when they are espoused with seemingly minimal reflection or
self-criticism.

One of the key questions in Christian youthwork concerns
the means by which young people are changed by their encounter with God. Youth ministry has developed three
separate lines of thought on this issue. Each of us will tend to
favour one of these approaches over the others and our
ministry will be shaped by this understanding of change.

The Holy Spirit Changes People

The fully blown charismatic tendency is to turn at every
occasion to miraculous intervention. The techniques and skills
of youth ministry are thus regarded as being somewhat unspiritual and basically irrelevant. According to this view the
crucial thing is that we worship God and we invite the Spirit
to come and meet us.

Stories from this approach to youth ministry tend to emphasize the unintentional nature of God's miraculous intervention. Despite our lack of knowledge of what is happening in a young person's life, the Spirit has led us to pray the right prayer or say the right prophetic words. At the same time evangelism can be reduced to involvement in worship – if we can get the non-Christian into the worship service then they will encounter God with power and that will change them.

The Word Changes People

In response to the growth in charismatic spirituality, conservative evangelicalism has tended to become more strident. In contrast to a Spirit-led miraculous expectation, these Christians emphasize the importance of the preaching of the word. The view is that the Christian gospel is essentially a message which young people need to hear and respond to. The key to successful and faithful Christian youthwork is therefore the presentation of truth. The gospel can be expressed in a set of propositions which are to be treated as absolute objective truth.

Young people are changed by hearing the word of God and responding to what they hear. The word of God must be accepted, and human sin and inadequacy must be acknowledged as a hindrance to the successful working of grace in our lives. This process is from beginning to end a rational discourse. Preaching is a means of sharing ideas concerning God. Young people for their part must respond to these ideas by coming to terms, rationally, with their own sinfulness. Commitment therefore becomes a matter of deciding to follow Christ.

Young People are Changed through Youthwork as Process

For many Christians the practice of youthwork has meant the discovery of particular approaches to informal education, community work, empowerment or counselling theory. Drawing on methodologies for social and individual change, Christians have adopted and adapted these practices. Change, according to these procedures, depends upon the energy of individuals and communities to set about changing themselves. Youthwork aims to provide a forum within which young people can gain an increased understanding of their own situation and the wider society. The Christian youthworker sets these issues within the context of the work of God in the world. It is when the Spirit of God begins to move young people to demand change in their own lives and at a grass roots level in their community that the kingdom comes into being. The key to this is young people discovering their own ability to change.

These three portraits are of course caricatures. Youth-workers in practice will adopt one or more of these approaches at the same time. But whatever approach or combination of approaches is adopted there is a need for theological reflection upon the action and work of the Holy Spirit to inform youth-work.

The Spirit, as we have seen, is involved with all aspects of the gospel story. Creation is brought about by the action of the Spirit. This means that we must not play down the ability of young people to discover their own power. We are powerful and able to change because God has made us that way. The natural abilities of people are blessed by God's Spirit in the supernatural but also in natural ways. To regard insights and styles of work which are based on theories of individual and social change as somehow 'unspiritual' is to ignore the breadth of the Spirit's engagement with the world. At the same time those Christians committed to community work or informal education will need to develop an understanding of how God is at work in this process if it is to be understood as truly Christian. To admit the involvement of the Holy Spirit in social and individual change must leave us open to the super-natural, or the 'charismatic'. The Spirit moves in creation through both the natural and the supernatural. We cannot have one without the other. A Spirit who does not work wonders is less than God.

A theology of the word is essential. The word of God in Christian tradition has been regarded as the means by which God effects change in the world. It is the word of God in Isaiah which does not return without bringing into reality the wish of God (Isaiah 55.11). Evangelicals see the preaching of the word as the means by which people 'hear the good news'. Hearing the good news is essential to spiritual renewal.[14]

41

Evangelicalism has grown and developed out of this under-standing of spiritual change. We need to affirm that the gospel story speaks of a historic reality and that it is possible to speak with truth about the death of Jesus and humanity's need for repentance. The Holy Spirit is deeply involved with this pro-cess. It is the Spirit who is sent out in order that the death of Christ can become a reality in people's lives. For it is through the Spirit that we experience grace. The Spirit quickens our hearts to respond as we ought to the gift of life. Yet the Spirit also is at work through the human techniques and insights of youth ministry. To focus exclusively upon the reception of the word of God as the means of learning and change is to reduce the Spirit, and make idols of our understanding and hearing. Similarly the miraculous and powerful intervention of God in our lives must not be discounted or put down. The God of the gospel story is disruptive and disturbing. He is not reducible to a set of objective absolutes. The charismatic intervention of the Spirit speaks of the ability of God to defy our neat categories.

The energy and life which is sweeping through charismatic congregations and churches at the present time is extremely exciting. Our enthusiasm for the dramatic intervention of God in the lives of young people is well-founded, but we need to allow for the possibility that the Holy Spirit is broader than the purely miraculous. While encounter with God in wor-ship and ministry is profound and valuable, youth ministry from within the charismatic tradition needs to take the process of education, growth and development amongst young people seriously. The Holy Spirit in the gospel story interacts with creation without doing violence to its essence. Creation is brought into being through the activity of the Spirit. This per-spective needs to temper the enthusiasm for the miraculous amongst charismatic groups. Similarly the realization that it is not only possible but can be 'Spirit inspired' to think rationally about the Christian faith must not be lost in the current scene.

3

The Incarnational Approach

RELATIONSHIPS ARE THE fuel on which youthwork travels. For the nucleus model the relational energy which makes the approach work is primarily supplied by young people who share their faith with their friends. In the incarnational approach relationships are also very much to the fore. In this case, however, we are talking of the relationship between Christian adults and young people. This chapter explores how relationships between young people and youth ministers change and develop as ministry amongst unchurched young people evolves. A pattern for working outside-in is presented. In the last part of the chapter these insights are applied to work which is inside-out.

To be engaged in building relationships with young people is an intentional activity. We choose to move beyond what we would consider to be our usual friendship groups and social contacts to make a connection with young people. Our presence amongst a group of young people is an 'intervention' in that we have crossed a natural social boundary in order that we might bring about change in the lives of young people. We might understand this change as empowerment, or helping, or even in more social terms as building relationships, or we might express our reason for crossing the boundary as a desire to share the Christian faith. However we express our motivation for doing youthwork, we must accept the inevitable artificiality of what we are doing. Given the normal course of events we would not make such intimate connections with a group of young people. The only reason we are in relationship is because we are Christian youthworkers, that is we believe that we have been called by God to engage in sharing the gospel. The incarnational discipline of youth ministry, like any other approach to youthwork, needs to recognize

43

that it is an activity which is out of the ordinary. It is for this reason that it is imperative that we are clear in our own minds what exactly we are involved in. Chapter 2 explored the theology of youthwork, this provides a set of values and some idea of the style of our involvement with young people. In addition to this there is also a need to be able to express a basic plan of how we envisage our work amongst young people growing and developing into the future. Without such a plan we are likely to fall foul of several problems which are often associated with youthwork.

First, we could very easily lose our way in the work we are doing. A lack of direction in the work will not only mean that we will not be successful in being good news amongst young people, it could also mean that we disappoint those who support our work. If we are voluntary or full-time workers, we have a duty to those who pray for our work, to those who make up our management committees, or to the local church which encourages us to work with young people. If we are able to express our aims and objectives clearly, then those around us are able to hold us accountable for the progress of the work and we are also able to assess how we are doing. Second, if we are clear in our own minds how we hope to see the work develop, then we will be less vulnerable to the influence that our own personality will have upon the work. Youthwork must be 'safe'; we must remain certain that we are not engaging in youthwork primarily to satisfy our own need for sexual fulfilment, emotional security, power or significance. Youth ministers are called to be good news amongst young people not bad news.

We are bad news when our own lack of self-awareness leads us to abuse young people emotionally, physically or spiritually. The key to avoiding such abuse will lie primarily in our own integrity and in a context in which we are held to account by people with whom we talk through what we do in the work. Every youthworker should have an agreed pattern of supervision for the work they are doing with young people. Patterns of supervision vary from organization to organization. For the purposes of this discussion, however, the key point is that all workers, voluntary or full-time, must have a formal contract to meet with a suitably qualified supervisor on a regular basis. This kind of supervision is a basic requirement of any work with young people. Alongside supervision we also need to keep in mind an agreed pattern for the work.[1]

A plan will help to identify when our own issues, needs and personality are starting to pull the ministry out of shape. The realistic youth minister will admit that it is not a question of 'if', it is more likely to be matter of 'when' or 'how' disastrously we go out of line. Supervision and an agreed plan for the work are necessary because we are engaged in complicated relationships which will from time to time need to be adjusted or brought back into line.

Third, we need to create a pattern for our ministry so that we are able to include others in the work. Youth ministry requires a team approach. In the first instance we may well have to start building relationships with young people on our own or in pairs. As the work progresses, however, it is vitally important that the number of adults involved in the work, either as volunteers or paid workers, is increased. Youth ministry which speaks of Jesus must model the community of faith. Young people in order to receive the fullness of the gospel need to see faith as a living reality in a number of different people's lives. A clear plan for the work enables others to understand how the work is going to progress. They can get a grip on how their part in the work might develop and how this links with the role they are playing at the present time. The plan also enables them to value the parts of the work with which they are not directly concerned. They are therefore more able to see the work as a whole and share in the overall vision.

A Model for Relational Outreach

The following pattern for working outside-in is based upon my own experience amongst young people in Oxford. The model is a summary of the different approaches to youthwork which have been developed by myself and others in Oxford Youth Works. After several years of experimenting with various approaches to youthwork, we have tried to sum up our work in five basic stages.[2] These five stages are a simplification of the route we have actually taken over the years. They are by no means a foolproof guarantee of success. Neither are they an infallible or unchangeable pattern of work. Rather they are regarded by myself and others in the team at Oxford Youth Works as a measure or guide for our work. We use this pattern as a starting point for our own creative attempts to reach out to young people. We have never wanted to feel that we are simply following a blueprint. In general we feel that the best youthwork has yet to be done.[3] In setting out this pattern I would therefore request that you attempt to treat the ideas in the same spirit. To the extent that it rings true then take it as guide, to the extent that it seems off-beam, feel free to treat it as a jumping-off point for you to do something which is more in keeping with your own situation.

Each of the five stages is described in terms of an answer to a question, how relationships between young people and youthworkers grow, a programme of activities and a spiritual challenge.

CONTACT

When I was working as a church-based youthworker, I was acutely aware that the young people I was meeting on a regular basis were all Christians. The structure of youth group meetings provided me with the only place where I met any young people at all. If a non-Christian came to the group then I could welcome them and try to get to know them. If for long periods none came, then I was evangelistically rather dormant. One solution was to try to encourage the group to invite their friends along by running a 'mission'. This strategy, however, seemed to still rely upon the Christian young people attracting their friends. Unfortunately my experience was that they seemed unwilling, or unable to attract non-Christians into the group. The nucleus approach was not working (or at least that was my perception at the time), what could I do? Was there a way of working which did not depend upon the group of young people who had grown up in the Church?

The question I started with was, 'How can I meet non-Christian young people?' The solution I quickly came to was that in order to meet groups of young people, I would have to find a way of going to the places where they naturally 'hung out'. My first choice was the local school. As a full-time youthworker I was available to visit at lunch-times. Through previous visits to the school I was aware that at that time there was a thriving culture of teenage bands. Music was one of my interests and so I devised a plan to get to know those pupils who were trying to get going in the music scene in Oxford. My plan was relatively simple: I went to the school and took an assembly. Working with the blessing of the music teacher and the headmaster I asked anyone interested in learning to play guitar, bass or drums to meet me at break-time in the hall. I also offered to come and meet up with any pupils who were starting to get bands together. That break-time I was swamped by young people all wanting to start learning to be rock stars. In addition to the large group of beginners there were also three young bands who came by to check me out. Over the next few weeks I tried to get to as many band rehearsals as I could. In addition to this I opened up a room at the school and started some basic guitar tuition.

My solution to the question 'How can I meet non-Christian young people?' is only one amongst many. I know of one place where for the last few years a group of volunteers have been going into the town centre on weekday nights to meet the young people who gather there. This is not a hard or tough city centre but a small town, where local young people who are at a loose end drift into the deserted precincts when they are too young to hang out in cars or get into pubs. Over a period of years these youthworkers have built caring and supportive relationships with these young people, acting as resources for advice and support at times of crisis. In recent times one of the young people has started to come along to church through the work of the group.

Sport is another good meeting point. There are many Christians who are deeply involved in the lives of young people because they are regularly acting as coaches with sports teams. Christians in Sport have developed an approach to relationship-based outreach which starts with the contact

Christian adults already have with groups of young people through sport. The programme is called Sports Plus.[4]

In many places groups of young people are all too evident. Some youthwork projects are started by churches because they can see that there are groups of young people hanging around on the streets, or even in the grounds of the church. Finding these young people may not be the problem, but there is still the question, 'How do I get to meet them?' Groups of young people do appear to be threatening or just a little unnerving to the average adult. The thought of going up to a group of young people outside the fish and chip shop is a very scary prospect. Contact work, however, is about the attitudes and skills which are necessary to move out from the relatively comfortable world of church-based youthwork into the ebb and flow of young people's lives.[5] For some of us this will mean finding shared activities or interests where we can start to build friendships with young people. For others of us it will mean finding ways to meet young people on the streets, in the shopping centre, or in the local parks. However we develop contact, the aim will be to build long-term relationships.

Contact is the very first stage in a complicated process of relationship-based youthwork. At its simplest level contact is the time when you first connect with a group. To make contact successfully we have to journey onto the territory of a group of young people. This means finding a place where a group of young people are at home and comfortable and going to that place to be with them. Most adult encounters with young people take place in a social context where the young people are at a disadvantage to the adults. The role and authority we have as adults generally safeguard us from exposure to the real social world of young people. When adults arrive on young people's territory, they often do so to tell them off or get them to clear out. The contact stage involves us in coming into social contact with individuals or groups of young people in ways that lay aside the normal adult authoritarian roles. We attempt to connect with young people in ways that do not impose our rules or guidelines upon them. Our first concern is that we are able to make a genuine connection which is based upon mutual respect and trust.

The starting point for this relational youthwork involves an uncritical position on the part of the adult youthworker. This does not mean that we will suspend our values or commitments as Christians. It means that when we first make connection with a group of young people, we accept them as they are. We are the visitors in their world and we will need to learn the correct way to relate. Our first priority is gaining some familiarity with the unwritten rules which govern the life of the group. We need to understand how the group works, who the leaders are and who the followers. Our starting point therefore must be one of being around the young people without trying to impose our values upon them. At times their behaviour may cause us some embarrassment or even place us in a compromising position morally or even legally. It is our task to maintain relationship but to do so without losing our integrity as youthworkers or Christians. This will mean that during the early stages of contact work there may be occasions when we will have to leave the group. At other times we will have to decide what kind of compromise we are willing to make in order to maintain relationship.

Contact work is first and foremost about spending time with a particular group of young people. The worker will need to make a regular commitment to building relationships. The frequency of meetings will, to some extent, depend upon the amount of time the young people themselves spend together. A football team which meets twice a week will require the worker to make contact on at least one of these meetings. A group in school which is together every break and lunch-time each school day will require at least three visits a week. The key is that enough time is spent in contact with the group so that the worker can become accepted as a regular and welcome visitor.

The youth minister needs to bear in mind at all times that he or she is engaged in building relationships as an adult. It is not our aim to become one of the gang. To seek acceptance as one of 'the lads' or 'the girls' is to defeat the object of our involvement. We are engaged in building relationships precisely because as adults we have something which is extremely valuable to offer to young people – friendship with a caring adult. If we sell out on our 'adultness' in any way, we lose our greatest asset.

Contact ministry is primarily about a low level engagement with a group of young people. The main activity involves being around the young people as they do the things which make up their everyday lives. It is hardly necessary to say terribly much. A relationship can start with a nod of the head or a smile. This however needs to lead on to more extended conversations as seems appropriate. It is very important not to try too hard. Artificial interaction is forced and comes over as adult control. We have the purpose of getting to know these young people but they may very well not share this agenda with us. We need to wait and hang about until the friendliness or curiosity of the group allows us to say something.

For those youth ministers involved in sporting, artistic, or musical activities the same kind of rules apply. When I was helping young people learn the guitar I saw it as being very important that I kept my organization of the activity to a minimum. The aim was to allow the young people space to get on with playing the instruments themselves. I would help out where I could, but on the whole I was just hanging around. I would wait for a chance to make conversation which came from the initiative of the young people themselves. Of course I had to keep a friendly and open manner – silence can be very intimidating. The occasional encouraging comment went a long way. I have to say that when it comes to contact work there can be a marked difference in working with boys or girls. Youth ministers who work with groups of girls seem to strike up significant relationships much more quickly. One reason for this is that conversation and the exchange of information can be much more free flowing with girls than boys.

Contact work is not for everyone. Making a connection with a group of young people outside a formal youthwork setting can be very demanding. A good rule of thumb for anyone considering this work is the level of sociability that is part of their everyday lives. If they are the kind of people who find themselves in conversation with people at the supermarket checkout or waiting to buy a ticket for the train, then they are a natural for a detached pattern of contact work. If conversations happen best when they are engaged in a shared activity with people then a more formal setting may be better suited to their personality.

Entering the social world of a group of young people is a spiritual journey. Youthwork therefore needs to start with a commitment to prayer and a belief that God is guiding the youthworkers in the relationships which they build. Prayer is therefore the basis for Christian youth ministry.

The acceptance which is a vital part of this first stage of work means that the youth minister should be continually looking for the way that God is leading them in relationships. This demands a spiritual insight into the way that the relationships develop. All the time the need for friendship must be tempered by a concern to remain faithful to Christian belief. Above all it is the Holy Spirit who opens doors into relationship with young people. Fundamental to the approach must be the realization that we do not take the Spirit to these young people. God is intimately aware of the young people's lives and he is already at work amongst them. The youthworker is a concrete sign of God's interest and presence. It is therefore vital to be spiritually in touch with the God whose nature is to reach out to young people.

Contact work takes the youth minister outside the prescribed arena of church-based work. Suddenly it is not at all clear what the rules are. The worker is now a beginner learning the ropes. The experience of worship in church and even as youthworkers is no preparation for this kind of freewheeling role. Relationship with God is the key element in the work. In the first instance this means a commitment to search the scriptures continually for signs of how to engage in the lives of particular groups of young people we have got to know. The questions which the ministry raises need to be brought to the study of the Bible. This will sometimes mean that we search wider than the familiar proof text territory we may have been used to.

Setting out to meet young people should not be a 'lone

ranger' ministry. The youthworker is ministering amongst
young people as part of the Church. Every youthworker
should therefore try to have around them a group of Christians
who pray about the work. The group should serve as people
who share the fears, frustrations, joys and successes of the
work. This kind of fellowship expresses the ownership of the
whole Church of this aspect of mission in a local area. A praying
group also contributes to an atmosphere of spiritual energy
and accountability for the work.

EXTENDED CONTACT

Contact ministry is the bedrock upon which incarnational
work is based. There is no substitute for being around young
people on their own territory. The first stage of the work, however, should not be regarded as a temporary fishing trip to
start something with a group of young people. Neither should
it be seen as the whole of the work.

Some churches and youthworkers have invested heavily in
finding ways to meet young people. The purchase of a bus or
the starting up of a drop-in centre or an alcohol-free bar have
been ways that Christians have sought to develop contact
with young people. The problem in some of these cases is
that the work has not managed to move beyond the first level
of relationship building. Conversations between workers and
young people can remain on a fairly superficial level. The result
is that intimacy and sharing have sometimes failed to material-
ize. This may be due to a high turnover of young people. An
example of this would be ministry based on a mobile café
which parks down in the town centre every Saturday. This
kind of ministry may suffer from the infrequency with which
individual young people drop by the café. It is possible for a
young person who has seemed sociable one week to be
unfriendly the next or, more likely, not even show up. A similar
problem can arise from the turnover associated with volunteer
workers or the amount of time volunteers are able to offer. If
the worker, or in this case the mobile café, can only be around
once a week then the likelihood of significant relationships
being formed is very low.

Extended contact is therefore a stage in the work which

52

addresses the question, 'How can relationships between workers and young people deepen?'

Friendship happens as people do things together. When we
share experiences we develop intimacy. The key to moving
beyond the first stages of contact will therefore be finding a
natural and mutually rewarding way to spend more time with
the young people. It is essential that the youth minister does
not try to rush this stage of the work. There is no short cut to
developing a trusting and mutual relationship with a group of
young people. The clue to when it is right to try and move relationships forward will always come from the young people
themselves. It could be that they themselves issue an invitation.
For instance after long weeks continually discussing football
with a group the youthworker may well find himself invited
to go along to the next fixture. As one young person said to
me the other day, 'You go up the Manor?'[6] In some cases the
youthworker may initiate the visit – when the group starts to
discuss the forthcoming game, the youthworker could ask if
it is all right to come along.

Extended contact moves a relationship physically away from
the point of contact. This means that the group who meet at
the park go on a trip to the seaside. The group who sit in the
classroom go into town after school for a MacDonalds. By
being willing to do something with a group, the youthworker
is signalling that they are significant to him. The young people
for their part are expressing an acceptance of the youth minister
which goes beyond the casual meeting which has so far characterized the work. They may feel that the youthworker has so
far been just passing by, but now they are opened to new possibilities. From a closed horizon contact situation, the work has
opened up to seem full of possibilities.

Doing things with young people is not an end in itself. It is a
means to deepen relationships. In the first instance this will
happen because of shared experience. A good time will most
likely be remembered by all concerned. But perhaps more significantly extended contact allows for the young people and
the youth minister to get to know each other better. Conversations are sparked in the mini-bus or on the coach. Suddenly
the worker is able to speak at more length with individuals.

The realization that the youth minister is committed to the group will often spark questions such as 'Why do you do this?', 'Are you married?', 'How come you work for a church, do you believe it all then?', 'What if we came to church would they like us?' These kinds of conversations are the initial stages in a deepening relationship. They are generally not a challenge, but a genuine enquiry. The youthworker finds herself being checked out concerning most aspects of her life, from sex, to drug-taking, from where she lives and with whom, to what music she likes and why she wears such terrible clothes! For the youthworker the period of extended contact provides the opportunity to get a little deeper with individuals and the group as whole. Direct questions may be inappropriate, but there will be a need to go with the flow of what individuals bring up in conversations. The early stages of any conversation offer clues as to what we find important and what we would want to talk about more. It is the sensitive youthworker who follows these clues without putting people on the spot.[7]

Extended contact really can be anything. The key will be that it is something which interests the young people concerned and that it allows for some kind of deeper sharing. Some activities, however, are of limited worth, e.g. a rock concert. In my experience a visit to a gig with young people can be quite frustrating. There is little which can be shared when all you can do is yell as loud as you can into each others ears because the band have cranked up the amps and are going at it full pelt. However, the trip to the gig and after it (if you can still hear) can be extremely valuable. The concert gives a point of departure for conversation and a sense of having done something together.

Activities with young people fall into two categories. The first will be those situations where the group have decided to do something and the youthworker simply joins in. For instance a group may decide to meet up in town on a Saturday and check out the fashion shops, boys, etc. The youthworker may agree to be there and go along with the flow of the group's activities. In this situation the youthworker, while being an adult in the group, is not acting as organizer or *in loco parentis* (in place of parents). The status of this activity means that when problems arise the youthworker is not responsible in a technical sense; however, they will be expected to behave responsibly. For instance on a trip to town it might become apparent that some of the group are shoplifting or intending to shoplift. In this situation the first thing to bear in mind is that an adult accompanying the group has a responsibility to take some action. This probably does not mean turning the young people in to the security guard at the shop or reporting them to the police. Relationship should be maintained, while it is made clear that the youthworker cannot have anything to do with stealing. This is an appeal for the young people to understand that as an adult the youthworker has responsibilities and values. The youthworker is not saying that shoplifting is wrong, therefore they must stop doing it. The youthworker is saying, however, that shoplifting is wrong, and for my sake please don't do it. This is an appeal to relationship. If the relationships with the group are not strong, then the youthworker will not be successful. If contact work has been going on for a while, then the young people will be more likely to value the relationship with the adult and they will realize that what they are doing is 'out of order'. If the group are not willing to accept the youth minister's advice, as a last resort, the youthworker must leave the group to do what they have decided to do. It is important that the youthworker takes time to explain why he is taking this action.

There is a most important distinction to be made between a trip organized by a youthworker and an informal joint activity. The former involves a great deal more responsibility on behalf of the youthworker and an acceptance of the youthworker in that role on the side of the young people. This development represents a quantum leap in relationship. For the youthworker the shift is from informal hanging around a group, accepting the general flow of behaviour, the language and the rules of the group, to becoming an adult who dictates what the ground rules of the trip will be. For instance a trip in a mini-bus to visit the seaside involves a number of responsibilities on the part of the youthworker which means that she cannot 'go with the flow'. A trip of this sort with young people who are under the age of eighteen involves some kind of parental consent. This might mean a visit to the young people's homes to make sure that the parents or guardians are willing for them to come on the day trip. Insurance will generally mean that some kind of form is filled in. The youth minister will also have to follow the health and safety guidelines laid down by her organization, the local authority, or the church from whom she has hired the mini-bus.

The basic responsibilities involved in organizing a trip are an indication of a change in role for the youthworker, but more significantly the young people will need to come to terms with this new side to the youthworker's presence amongst them. A trip organized by the youthworker places her in the role of rule maker. For instance there is the question of the mini-bus. The worker cannot allow the bus to be trashed. The question of smoking on the bus may be raised. The hire company or the local church may have made it clear to the youth minister that smoking on the bus is not allowed. A crucial transition from contact ministry to extended contact work can be brought about by this kind of question. The youthworker has to act as a responsible adult and stick to the rules of hiring the mini-bus and risk the disapproval of the group. The only way forward is for the youthworker to negotiate with the young people. In many cases it is essential to discuss issues such as the problem of smoking on the bus with the group before the trip ever gets underway. The conversation could go something like this:

> **Youthworker:** There's a problem. We are not allowed to smoke on the bus.
> **Young People:** What?
> **YW:** Sorry, its the church's bus and they don't want it to smell like an ash tray on Sunday when they pick up the old folks.
> **YP:** Could we have a fag out the window? We could clear it up afterwards spray some of that air freshener around.
> **YW:** Look I promised the guy at the church no smoking and I don't want to let him down. What I thought is we could possibly have a fag break halfway, what do you think?

These kinds of discussions are the stuff of which youthwork is made.[4] Without such discussions the youth minister will never be accepted by the group as someone who can at times act as leader. Moreover the lack of a negotiated agreement on what passes for acceptable behaviour and what is out of order means that the youthworker may well be prevented from moving the relationship with the group on in the way that is hoped for and planned. It is a temptation to go with the energy of the young people and betray the trust of the Church. This might gain some short-term popularity with the group, but over the long-term it will undermine the role of the youthworker as a responsible adult and possibly as a herald of good news.

It is one thing to decide to be a youthworker, it can be quite another to build significant relationships with young people. Relationships bring with them spiritual responsibilities. More often than not contact with young people can be energizing and very rewarding. At times, however, they can also require us to be giving in very costly ways. Extended contact is the time when young people begin to open up about what their lives are really like. We get a much clearer picture of their hopes, fears, problems and hurts. To be a caring adult friend is a spiritual matter. It is the strength which our faith gives us which keeps us involved when the emotional cost can be very great. Prayer sometimes becomes a matter of daily survival. We need to seek God to try and make sense of what we are experiencing as well as to gain strength.

Extended contact is also the time when our Christian identity will be explored by young people. To be involved in building relationships as an aspect of mission means that we need to be ready to offer an account of why we are doing youthwork. It is vital that we are upfront and clear about who we are and what we are doing. To say that we are a youthworker attached to a church or Christian organization is generally a very acceptable explanation of what we are doing. The young people we are getting to know will discover this in the natural course of a deepening relationship. There is usually little to be gained from announcing to the group on first meeting them that we are 'Christians'. They will just conclude that we are weirdos from some kind of cult. Faith is a deep and intimate part of our identity and one which in the normal course of things generally comes into focus quite late in relationships. Our first priority should be to meet the young people as a trusting and trust-worthy person. Faith is integral to this for us, but the proof of the pudding is always in the eating, not the colour of the label.

Having said this we must also be very clear and honest about our Christian identity when we are asked. This might simply mean that when asked what we are doing on Sunday, we say we are going to church. To try to hide this in the belief that 'church' somehow makes us unacceptable to the group is a mistake. I have had cause to learn this over again with Nick Allen, one of my colleagues from Oxford Youth Works. Each week Nick takes some record decks into a local school to let a group of boys use them to mix records and rap to them. Nick regularly talks about how he uses the decks and the records in church. This fact is accepted with very little comment, if any, by the group, it is just a fact of life when hanging out with Nick.

Nick was also the one who suggested to me that extended contact might be the time to begin to talk to young people about Jesus. He has tried on a few occasions to tell Bible stories as part of normal conversation. The idea is that the Christian youthworker follows the example of Jesus in being someone who tells stories about the kingdom. Nick says that on one occasion when he was in a pub he started to tell a Bible story to make a point in the conversation. People were leaning across the table to catch the drift of the story, such was their interest. Extended contact therefore is the time when some explicit sharing of the faith might start to take place as and when it seems appropriate. In this way the gospel message does not appear just as an agenda item further down the track without any introduction.

Another way of making this kind of connection with young people is to invite them to come along to a Christian event or worship time. The purpose in this would be to give some exposure to the Christian perspective of the youthworker. It is a way of starting a conversation rather than a means to a quick conversion. The likelihood is that most young people will find a church service fairly unusual and maybe a little alienating. This need not be a problem if the youth minister is able to spend time listening to what the young people are saying and offer some explanation of what is going on.

PROCLAMATION

Extended contact is concerned with relationship building. During the period of extended contact we get to know a little more about the young people we are working with and they get to know us. They will experience the care which we see as the activity of God in their lives as a sign of grace whether they know it or not. There comes a time, however, when being and doing the gospel needs to lead on to telling the story. Christian mission needs to be concerned with the word of God proclaimed as well as with the word of God incarnated in our lives.

It is essential that Christian youthworkers take on board the challenge of finding an appropriate way to share the gospel story with young people. Telling the story will involve allowing space for young people to question what they have heard. This testing of the message is essential if young people are to get a handle on what the story is about and what it might mean if they were to become a part of it. We should also allow room within our proclamation of the story for young people to make a response to the God they are hearing about and who cares for them. Proclamation therefore answers the question, 'How do I share the Christian message with the young people I have got to know?'

Proclamation involves another crucial change in the dynamics of the relationship between the young people and the youth minister. The youthworker needs to come to terms with a movement from being an adult friend who occasionally organizes trips and events to being someone who overtly tells the gospel message. The young people for their part need to be willing to accept this change in role and allow space to hear what the youth minister is saying. This may sound very intimidating and something of a daunting prospect. The key, however, will generally lie in the extent to which the youthworker has established a caring and credible presence amongst the group of young people. The problem is that most of us have heard horror stories, or even played our part in horror stories where an evangelistic event has been wrecked by a group of unruly young people. An example of this would be the embarrassment of trying to conduct an epilogue at the end of an open youth club which may well be our only experience of trying to speak about Jesus to a group of unchurched young people. In most cases the young people and those doing the preaching in these situations do not know each other.

The kind of long-term relationship building which characterizes contact and extended contact means that the relationship dynamic is more established. Proclamation which follows a long-term involvement with a group of young people is very different from a club epilogue. Jim Rayburn, the founder of the American organization, Young Life (upon which much of this model is based), used to say that youthworkers should 'Earn the right to speak.'[8] By this he meant that we should have been around enough to be known and to get to know young people before we start talking about Jesus. Preaching the gospel without relationships between the preacher and the young people may be fine when we are working inside-out, since in most youth groups or churches the relational element needed for successful outreach has been provided by the friendship between Christian young people and non-Christians. Working outside-in means that the youthworker must provide the relational heart of the work.

The context in which we try to proclaim the gospel is very important. We may well only get one chance to speak in a more formal way about Jesus with a group of young people. If we blow it, it will take a good deal of work to get the group to a point where they will accept this kind of activity again. It is therefore very important to make clear to the young people what we have in mind. The youth minister needs to check out with them if it would be all right to do something which is a little more spiritual. A discussion could be based upon a previous experience, perhaps a visit to a church or the ongoing activity of telling stories about Jesus. In this way the idea could be presented as a question, 'How would you feel about doing something like the church service we went to but with better music?'

My own preferred approach to proclaiming the gospel has been to run a special holiday or trip away where it is clear that part of what goes on would involve an exploration of the Christian faith. This should be fully explained ahead of time so that the young people can choose to sign up if they feel comfortable with the idea. The spiritual nature of the holiday should also be set out in any publicity material used to promote the event. It is vital that it is made clear that there is no pressure to decide to become Christians. The main purpose of the holiday would be to inform and allow the young people to make up their own minds on the basis of what they have heard.

The actual sharing of the gospel story needs to be thought through in some detail. On the one hand, it is crucial that the young people are told the whole story in sufficient depth for them to grasp what the Christian message is about. On the other, these will not be university theology lectures or even church sermons. There is a need for the youthworker to bear in mind the life experiences and social context of the group. On the basis of this a number of stories, primarily about Jesus, need to be chosen which unlock the meaning of the gospel and which shed light on their normal lives. I have found a pattern for evangelistic talks based on those used by Young Life to be very helpful:

● Start with an experience of the young people themselves.
● Tell a relevant story about Jesus.
● Link the experience of the group and the Bible story.
● Explain what this means for the young people.
● Shut up.

This pattern is repeated over five days with the youthworker covering basic topics such as: Who was Jesus? What did he say? What did he do? Why did he die? and How can we meet him today?

The reality is that when we move to this stage of the work we step into the unknown with the group in a way which we

have never done before. There is often a spiritual barrier which
youthworkers experience when they contemplate speaking
clearly about the Christian message. Sometimes this can be
because of a lack of confidence in our ability to tell the gospel
story. This may mean that the youthworkers will need to take
it on themselves to rehearse what they are going to do or get
some formal training in sharing the gospel. It is also possible
that the youthworkers have a lack of faith that telling the message of Christ will have any effect upon a particular group of
young people. This is an important spiritual challenge which
needs to be overcome. There may be no substitute for just
taking our life in our hands and telling the story to a group of
young people. It is possible, however, that we can gain some
confidence by recalling the power that the message about
Jesus has had on us in the past or upon people we know. The
gospel is a powerful message because it is rooted in God's
love for us. Youthworkers need to grasp this with a confidence
which can only come by continual prayer and worship.

NURTURE

It is when young people respond to the gospel that the really
demanding work starts. For youthworkers working outside-
in, the problem of Christian nurture is not solved by an existing
church-based nucleus group which can slowly socialize the
young people into the faith. The most likely situation is that a
small group of young people will want to explore the implications of the Christian faith in more depth. The question
which relates to this stage therefore is, 'How do we help
young people learn about the faith outside an already existing
Christian group?'

The youth minister is now in a very difficult position in
relation to the group. In the early stages he has been mainly
playing the role of learner. The temptation is for the youth
minister to start to see himself as the teacher, but this would
be a mistake. The aim of the nurture stage is to see a group of
young people start to explore the Christian faith themselves.[9]
The end result will be a group of young people who are able
to be truly Christian and yet also remain in contact with their
neighbourhood and their existing friendship group. We are

hoping that the faith can become real within their own sub-cultural setting. This means that while the youthworker may know more about the details of the Christian faith, he will not necessarily be able to make the connection between the Christian gospel and the community life of the young people.

In this situation the youth minister should act as a resource person using his experience and knowledge of the Bible and the Christian tradition to find material which might be most appropriate to the group. The role of the youthworker in this situation is primarily to act as someone who 'translates' biblical stories or insights from church history and theology into the present-day context of the group. This aspect of nurture and of church is explored more deeply in Chapters 5 and 7.

The youthworker tells stories and offers insights from her own experience and study. This material needs to be worked on by the young people to see how it makes sense for them. The most important thing is that the youthworker allows space for the young people to discuss the material and connect it with their lives. Bob Mayo says of his experience working amongst what he calls 'pre-nonchristian young people' in Bermondsey that he soon discovered that explaining the biblical stories was a mistake.[10] He had to be willing to tell the story from the Bible and allow the young people to make sense of it in their own terms. The key factor in this, according to Bob, is that young people from an unchurched background do not have the language to understand our explanations. The material from the Bible, on the other hand, is the raw stuff of revelation. The important thing is to try and make sure that our interpretation of the Bible does not get in the way of young people working it out for themselves. It is the youth minister's role to create safe places where young people can explore the Christian faith.

Nurture will generally involve some kind of group work. Young people who have decided to follow Jesus need a place where they can think in more depth about their decision. In the first instance many young people will have no idea how to pray, or how they should read the Bible, if indeed they read at all. The nurture group therefore needs to focus upon communicating not just the information about God, but also to teaching spiritual skills such as methods of prayer, discussion and worship.

Nurture should offer a chance for discussion. In some cases this will happen in a formal group and therefore needs to be facilitated in some way or another. In many cases conversations about faith will begin to permeate the activities which are more readily associated with contact and extended contact work. Nurture in this sense begins to look a little more like the kind of relationship Jesus developed amongst his disciples, with questions and answers, stories and explanation arising as the disciples accompanied Jesus on journeys or at meal-times.

It is important to try and bridge the gap between young people and the Church. As nurture starts to develop some attempt should be made to make the young people aware of the kind of worship and fellowship which exists in local churches. It might be that full membership of a church is a little ambitious for the group. However it is very important not to build any artificial barriers. Even more important the youthworker needs to make clear that what happens amongst the young people is very much connected to the wider Church.

Young Christians need constant support and help if they are to grow in the faith. The youth minister needs to build a community base where the young people can feel a sense of security without being forced into a churchy mould. This means that those involved in helping the group to explore the faith need to allow the young people to run the nurture group in a way which is most sensitive to the culture of the young people attending it. This includes the way that God is spoken about, how prayers, worship and the social activities which surround the group must all be based within the subcultural milieu of the group.

A sensitivity to culture and to the breadth of the Christian faith requires a certain degree of theological sophistication. This kind of work is essentially a missiological task of contextualization.[11] At a spiritual level the workers need to keep in mind that it is the Spirit of God who will lead the young people into truth. It is important to be able to operate outside the more familiar framework which offers a greater degree of certainty in a church context. The ambiguity of trying to leave space for young people to explore the faith for themselves needs to be balanced with some idea of the limits of Christian expression and interpretation. The judgements involved in deciding what is inside the possible limits of experimentation and what is outside are far from simple. Youthworkers need to be theologically informed and spiritually sensitive.

CHURCH

As Phil Moon says the Church is not an option for young Christians, it is part of the basic package.[12] This is the case whether we work inside-out or outside-in. The Church is the basic unit of Christian community which we are part of through our faith encounter with Christ. Our belonging to the Church is first and foremost a spiritual matter. The question is how we work this out in terms of groups of people and organizations. The nucleus approach to youthwork assumes the local church as a given reality. Working outside-in means that we have to find a solution to church for the young people we have got to know. The question for this stage is, 'How can the young people who have come to faith find a place in the Church?'

It may be possible for groups of young people to fit in with the life of a local congregation. This may, however, not be possible or desirable. In some cases young people will want to worship in ways which reflect their own subculture, and this will be different from that which happens in the church. In most cases a new congregational service will need to be formed to offer a church setting for the young people. This may well be linked to a local church or denominational group, but it will also need to establish a measure of independence. Either way young people who have found faith in Christ need to find a place within the Christian community.

In some cases it will be important for the youthworker and other young adults to sign up to this community in some way. The young adults and the youthworkers can then offer a strong network within the community formed around the young people. The relationship at this point begins to move towards a more independent or interdependent contact between youthworker and young people. The context of the community ideally should offer a place where youthwork as such comes to an end and an ongoing life in the church context might start. This may not be possible, however. There is some evidence that young people involved in a new worship service will eventually decide to find their own direction independent of youthworkers, however relational they may be. The role of worship and a church fellowship is therefore to provide enough experience of the faith for young people to decide in their own time what direction they will take. Youthwork should never seek to control young people, simply to offer choices. The church stage is no different in this respect.

Youthwork has as its goal the desire for young people to become independent of the youthworker. Christian youthwork will aim to offer the gospel as the context within which adult life should be lived. The move towards independence, however, may not come about without some confusion and frustration on the part of the young people and the youthworkers. If the youthworker is too directive, independence may well be delayed or may not even be achieved. This kind of dependence can be religious abuse. If, on the other hand the youthworker places the responsibility of the work in the hands of the young people the church may well descend into chaos. A balance between these two approaches is the best policy. One way of achieving this is to work with a team of helpers and the group of young people, so that the gifts needed to get the church off the ground can be found in more than one person. The problem with this, however, is that young people will still look to the youthworker they have known over a period of time for guidance and help. Relationships begun through contact and extended contact work should, if possible, be continued into the church setting.

The main activities of the church stage will be shaped by a desire to express a corporate Christian life within the subculture of the group. In many ways the life of the group at this stage will be little different from any other church congregation. The key, however, will be to seek a new way of being church with each other. This involves imagination and creativity. These issues are examined in more depth in Chapter 7.

The Church is called to be a foretaste of the kingdom of God. This means that the life of the group should be built around a desire to express in community life the values and concerns of God. Young people who have been fairly introverted within their own subculture will be challenged to open up their group life to other people. Not least, the community will need to express its unity with other Christians in churches and congregations locally. Where the young people's expression of church is linked to one local church, this openness to other Christians is particularly important. The challenge to be a community of faith will be a struggle. The biblical picture of the Church as the body of Christ, a community of priests and a building resting on the work of Christ should offer models for the development of church life amongst young people.

The challenge of a Christian community is to work with the biblical demand that we are to be a holy people, set apart by God. The life of the group therefore needs to move from the acceptance of any kind of lifestyle and behaviour which is common in most youth cultures to one which wrestles with the ethical demands of the gospel. To follow Christ together is to accept that he has a say in the way we live our lives. The new congregation will very soon need to work with these issues if it is to survive. The temptation is to accept everything and everyone unquestioningly. This is a mistake. On the other hand, there is the possibility that the youth minister and other church leaders may impose a set of standards upon the group which are inappropriate and insensitive. It is important to recognize that this kind of problem has been faced by the Church before. When the gospel was first preached to the Gentiles the predominantly Jewish Church needed to decide if the new Christians should be expected to follow the whole of the Jewish law or some part of it. Acts 15 records how the apostles and the elders of the Jewish Church, after much deliberation, came to agreement on this issue eventually deciding that full compliance with the Jewish law was not necessary for Christian discipleship in a Gentile context. However, two laws were laid down: the new Christians should refrain from eating meat which had been sacrificed to idols, and they should keep a rule of chastity. The present-day Christians have a similar role to that of the Jewish Church in working with groups of young people from subcultures so far outside the Church. Over time the new church will need to come to terms with difficult moral and ethical issues which arise within their own subculture. The wider Church will be a resource in helping these decisions to be made the best way possible.

Using the Model with a Nucleus Group

The pattern of contact work, extended contact, proclamation, nurture and church is really not very different for working with a church-based nucleus group. It is possible to see the nucleus group as contributing the proclamation, nurture and church aspects of the pattern. This means that to complete the plan a church-based youthworker needs to find ways of doing contact work and extended contact as a feed into an existing group.[13]

The key to developing contact work as a means to make a nucleus group more evangelistic lies in the young people with whom the youthworker aims to work. It is a temptation for the youthworker to be drawn to the more challenging 'frontier' kinds of young people. As youthworkers we often have a heart for young people who are hurting or for young people we consider to be at risk. The problem with this is that if we are also committed to running youthwork in a church, we soon find ourselves operating the two disciplines at the same time. Some youthworkers are talented enough to bridge this gap, but very few of us have the time or energy to run two different patterns of ministry. Time constraints probably mean that we should look for ways of doing contact work which complement the nucleus group. This means that we should look to be making relationships with young people who we can see will eventually fit in with the existing group.

One way to build the life of the nucleus group is to develop the contact work around the young people who already come to the church group. This means setting up informal contact in schools where the Christian young people are pupils, hanging out with them at lunch-times or when they are involved in activities such as sport or musical interests. The aim of this will be to try and supplement the relational outreach of the nucleus group by being another Christian presence around the young people and their friends.

Extended contact can then be a programme of mixed activities with both Christian and non-Christian young people. The value of being involved in the lives of the Christian young people is not just evangelistic. My own experience of running a church youth group made me feel that in many ways when I was trying to teach the group from the Bible I had to guess what their lives were like. Contact work means that the youthworker has a much more acute sense of the day-to-day reality of being a Christian in school and in the other areas of teenage life.

Contact work off the edge of a nucleus group means that the youthworker is able to welcome fringe members into the life of the group more effectively because they are likely to be known. The other advantage is that fringe members may come to one or more meetings and then drop away. Contact work offers a chance for the youthworker to informally discuss with the young person what they thought of the group and maybe find out what was going on. The dynamics of young people's lives mean that the reasons why people come to groups or stop coming maybe more to do with a social situation than with a spiritual decision, e.g. the young woman who comes to the group because she fancies one of the existing members; if the relationship doesn't work out the girl may feel embarrassed to continue coming to the group. Contact work means that the youthworker is not left helpless in a sea of changing hormones. There is the chance to follow up with fringe members and try to find a way round the problems.

Extended contact may also find a place in the life of a nucleus group. Working with an existing friendship group of nucleus members and non-Christians, activities can be devised which build a group feel and intimacy. The important thing, however, is that these extended contact activities always build into the life of the nucleus group and do not develop a life of their own.

4

Popular Culture

AN UNDERSTANDING OF culture is basic to Christian youthwork. It is fairly obvious that young people live and breathe
their own youth cultures. Communication of any sort therefore
involves some appreciation of this cultural world. Our work
generally involves some understanding of concepts of popular
culture and youth subcultures. Youth ministry is shaped by
youth culture, but it is also shaped by the culture of the Church.
This means that Christian youthworkers are culturally bi-
lingual – we understand and communicate, not only with
young people, but also with churches and Christian organizations. Standing between young people on the one hand and
the Church on the other, we are aware that both have
subcultures all their own. The affiliation which develops
around Christian music, language and church life has much in
common with the pattern of life we see amongst groups of
young people. Thus whether we are working in the Church
inside-out, or whether we are working in the community outside-in, the Christian youthworker needs to have developed a
relatively sophisticated understanding of the issues concerning
culture.

Current thinking concerning culture, popular culture and
subcultural theory is somewhat confused and complex.
Theories of the importance and function of culture and subcultures vary. This material is important for Christian youthwork because how we view culture will affect how we work,
both in relation to the Church and young people. This chapter
sets out a framework for the youthworker's encounter with
culture and suggests how particular theoretical perspectives
will impact the practical outworking of ministry amongst
young people.

High Culture and Popular Culture

The idea of culture has tended to carry with it a certain elitism.[1] It is common to regard some people as being 'cultured'. By this it is meant that they attend the right kind of artistic events and read the right kind of books. According to this view a visit to the opera is culture, but a Spice Girls or Boyzone concert is not. Cultured people read Dickens, but those who are not read Barbara Cartland. High culture is something we aspire to or improve ourselves with. It carries the deepest of human values, it is civilizing and spiritual. An appreciation of high culture is therefore regarded as basic to education. Young people are taken on organized trips to see plays by Shakespeare or to classical concerts and art galleries. High culture is part of our heritage to be subsidized by the government and preserved for the nation in art galleries and museums.

There are certain affinities between high culture and religion. It is possible to see the Christian faith as part of this cultural heritage. Church culture has its own contribution to make to the cultural make-up of our country. The Book of Common Prayer, the King James version of the Bible, church music and architecture are themselves high culture. The Church in this sense is a cultural repository, an approved and improving experience. If we embrace an élitist view of culture then we will expect young people to be educated into an appreciation of the cultural riches of the Christian faith as part of evangelism. Involvement in religious activity will demand considerable discipline and application on the part of young people. This kind of assumption has formed the implicit backdrop to a good deal of the Church's youthwork. Through choirs, bell ringing and serving in the liturgy many young people have been introduced both to the culture of the Church and to the Christian faith. The problem is that faith as the embodiment of high culture does not especially value the culture that young people bring to the Church. The expectation is that through a process of affiliation and education, young people will take on the values and sensitivities of the Church aesthetic and through this come to an appreciation of the spiritual values which are the reason for church music, architecture and liturgy.

Alongside the élitist understanding of culture as high culture there has also been a tradition associated with anthropology which is more inclusive. Definitions of culture within anthropology vary, but their common characteristic tends to be a desire to include all human behaviour and production. Thus culture includes: human knowledge, belief, art, morals, law, custom, economic relationships, myths and stories, sexual behaviour, in fact any aspect of life which is common to members of a society. A shorthand term from the discipline of anthropology would be that culture is 'all learned human behaviour'.[2] Learned behaviour is the cultural environment within which members of a society are born and live out their lives. Learned behaviour, culture, is therefore everything which binds a society together and makes it work. The idea that different societies have different cultural frameworks and worldviews is a key anthropological perspective. Within the theology of mission this kind of insight has been readily adopted. Christian missionaries have long been aware that their understanding of the faith is shaped within a Western cultural framework. The starting point for modern missiology therefore has generally been a desire to understand the culture of the people whom they are seeking to reach.[3]

Mission theology has developed a sophisticated understanding of the process whereby the gospel moves from one cultural framework to another. This process is described as contextualization or inculturation. These perspectives and their relevance to Christian youth ministry will be treated in more depth in the next chapter. It is important at this time to note the limitations of the anthropological view of culture for youth ministry. The overview of culture provided by anthropological definitions tends to foreshorten the tensions and cultural plurality within Western societies. A macro-view of culture as all things learned flattens out the subtle divisions between youth subcultures, racial groups, the impact of the media and a mass popular culture and indeed the presence of a vibrant church subculture. Youth ministry therefore should learn from the contextualizing understanding of mission which has grown within mission studies, but it also needs to draw more deeply from current debates concerning the nature and creation of popular culture(s) within our own society.

Current understanding of popular culture has grown from a debate concerning the significance of the impact of the media and 'mass culture'. For early critics the media was seen as the means whereby the interests associated with business and industry manipulated the 'masses' by the use of popular forms of entertainment. Popular culture was viewed with considerable suspicion because it was the means whereby capitalist interests controlled the majority of the population. Karl Marx stated that those who owned industry also controlled the means of cultural production. This interpretation was widely accepted in the 'culture industry' understanding of popular or mass culture. Religion may have declined in significance, so now it is television which has become the opiate of the masses. The emphasis upon amusement inherent within the mass media, it was argued, was there to stave off possible rebellion and social discontent. Mass culture is irretrievably imbued with the values of dominant groups in society. The masses, as they consume mass culture, are in the thrall of the values which support those with privilege. This critique of the culture industry is also essentially élitist. There are those who are in control, the élite, and there are those who are being brainwashed by television and the film industry. The brainwashed are regarded as entirely passive in the process. They are not communities or groups with a name and a life of their own. They are 'the masses' at the mercy of big business and the media.

In contrast to élitist views of the culture industry or the high culture understanding of culture there has developed an appreciation of the way by which people create their own cultures. This activity has generally been referred to as 'popular culture'. Through the work of E. P. Thompson, Richard Hoggart and Raymond Williams an understanding of culture which is rooted more firmly in the everyday lives of people has been introduced.[4] Culture in this sense is no longer simply the preserve of an educated élite. In the words of Raymond Williams, 'Culture is ordinary.' By this he means that the language,

songs, customs, games, sports and festivities which characterize working people's lives are themselves a tradition which is
filled with meaning. To understand culture in this sense is to
begin to value a much broader variety of activities and cultural
products as forming identity and carrying community values.
Hoggart and Williams were concerned to draw a distinction
between the traditional culture of the English working-class
and the imported 'mass culture' which was being peddled by
the media. The fear of 'Americanization' which came with the
post-war emergence of youth culture and the popularity of television and films was seen as being a significant threat to
home-grown culture. Popular culture for Williams, Thompson
and Hoggart was therefore a fairly romantic construction. As
the importance of the media grew in working people's lives,
the understanding and interpretation of popular culture needed
to take a more positive view of 'mass' culture. This perspective
was provided by the growth of cultural studies.

Cultural studies was put on the map in this country by the
work of the Centre for Contemporary Cultural Studies
(CCCS) at Birmingham University.[5] The Centre was originally
set up by Richard Hoggart, but his work was taken further by
Stuart Hall who along with a number of others started a programme of studying the meanings behind aspects of popular
culture. Central to this project was primarily the study of
television and then youth culture. The study of youth culture
therefore provides a useful introduction to the main findings
of cultural studies.

Subculture

Anthropological insights tend to treat culture as a single uni-
fied system of meaning. The concept of subculture, however,
is based upon the realization that 'learned behaviour' depends
upon the context within which that learning takes place.
Societies are divided by a number of inequalities. Traditionally
sociology has described these inequalities in terms of race,
gender and social class. These 'strata' give shape to the variety
of opportunity and community identity which individuals
experience in life. Who we are is fundamentally shaped by the

community within which we learn behaviour. We make sense of our identity and our place in the larger societal system on the basis of our location in the various strata.[6] Thus a young Asian woman growing up in Southall may well inhabit a very different subcultural world to a that of a young white man growing up in the leafy suburbs of Croydon.

For Stuart Hall and those in the CCCS the concept of subculture was used to explain the existence of 'resistant cultures' within society. Drawing on the work of the Italian theorist, Antonio Gramsci, Hall argued that culture provided an arena within which different groups in society carried out a struggle. Those groups which are economically and socially dominant seek to extend their authority by using culture to support their power. Culture then becomes a means for dominant groups in society to seek the assent of subordinate groups. When this assent is achieved it is called 'hegemony' by Gramsci. At the same time subordinate groups use the cultural arena as a means to create pockets of resistance. Hall combined these insights from Gramsci concerning culture as an arena for struggle with the theories concerning culture as a series of signs and symbols which was developed by the French philosopher Roland Barthes. Hall understood youth culture as an attempt to resist hegemony by creating subcultures. These subcultures are created by the use of particular kinds of dress, ways of behaving and ways of speaking which are laden with symbols and signs. The analysis of signs and symbols found in Barthes was used as the means to understand the meaning of youth subcultures such as 'punk' or 'mod'. The symbols when correctly understood reveal a style of life which is an attempt to create identity apart from that offered by the dominant culture. It is therefore 'resistant'.[7]

At the CCCS various youth subcultures were seen as the cultural products of mainly working-class young people. In the book *Resistance through Rituals* the style of Mods, Skinheads and other teenage groups are said to reveal symbolic meanings which point to 'contradictions' in society. In the case of Skinheads the contradiction experienced was seen as the erosion of traditional working-class communities. The widespread growth in unemployment was aggravated by the influx of Asian people newly arrived from India, Pakistan and Bangladesh. The response of working-class young people was to create a distinctive style which included 'bovver boots', braces and a shaven head. This style was seen by the authors of *Resistance through Rituals* as signifying a desire to return to pure working-class roots. By developing distinctive ways of dress, music and behaviour, young people are able to make 'cultural space' for themselves. In this cultural space they find meaning and identity over and against the dominant culture. The dominant culture might view Skinheads as hooligans and thugs, but the young Skinhead will see himself as 'cool' and 'hard'. To be cool and hard is to assert the right to an identity which is achieved through membership of the informal sub-cultural group rather than through conformity to the wider society.

The key interpretative framework used to understand youth subculture in *Resistance through Rituals* was social class. Youth culture was seen as the means whereby working-class young people who were considered disadvantaged, economically, educationally and socially achieved a sense of identity and therefore resistance. The book, however, was criticized for a reading of youth subculture based exclusively upon social class, most notably by Angela McRobbie. McRobbie argued that the reading of youth subcultures adopted by Hall and others tended to focus upon young men. The place of subculture within the lives of young women remained largely hidden. McRobbie has developed this insight, and in her later books *Gender and Generation* and *Feminism and Youth Culture*, she has sought to shed light upon the way that women use shopping as a means to create identity and meaning.[8] McRobbie's understanding of popular culture rather than being expressed in terms of the hegemonic struggle between social classes has been framed by a feminist understanding of society which is shaped by male patriarchy. Young women, she argues, are faced with a need to negotiate their sense of identity and worth in relation to the dominant view of women which is presented in advertising, TV shows and magazines such as the once popular *Jackie*.

Michael Brake extended the study of youth culture by studying not only working-class groups but also middle-class ones. He points out how the middle-classes have had a tradition of bohemian artistic lifestyles which have developed subcultures which are themselves 'counter-cultural' and resistant to the dominant culture. An example would be the 1960s hippie movement which was almost exclusively middle-class in origin. Whether working-class or middle-class, Brake points out that the attempt to create subcultures by young people is usually temporary and unsuccessful. The reason for this is that the 'contradictions' in society which have given rise to the creation of the subculture are only resolved at a cultural level. The initial sparking point in the creation of a subculture, he argues, will generally be economic, e.g. the fact that black young people in Britain experience disadvantage in getting jobs. Looking good and having the right haircut may bring a measure of self-respect and group identity, but it does not solve the real problem of the lack of adequate or suitable employment.

The meaning of subcultural style may be more than the creation of group identity. Dick Hebdige, writing as punk began to appear on our streets, saw style as a means to generate shock. Young people according to Hebdige create new subcultures by the creative bringing together of symbolic ways of dressing. Hebdige uses the term 'bricolage' to describe the chaotic combination of items of dress. The new combination carries with it the associations and meanings of each of the items of dress. By bringing together disparate items these meanings are disassociated from their original context and re-located within a new identity. Thus in punk, bondage gear usually associated with sexual fetish and hidden in the private world of sado-masochism, was used as an everyday fashion item, combined with mohican hair cuts and tartan kilts. Subcultural style thus becomes a means to disturb and create questions rather than the usual role of dress to reassure and locate individuals and groups within an understood social structure. Style is therefore a means to wage war on the public by the use of disturbing combinations of symbols and signs.[9]

Hebdige identified the crucial role played by those who were in the vanguard of the creation of particular subcultural styles.

It is to these groups where a style first emerges, argues Hebdige, that the cultural analyst is to look for meaning. Crucial to the original creation of subcultures and styles is the way that white young people interact with subcultures which have emerged within black communities, particularly in the United States. An example of this would be the way that working-class, white young people have in more recent times adopted the music, dress and the street language associated with rap and hip-hop which originally came from the urban Afro-American context. However, the spread of subcultural style, according to Hebdige, represents a slow disintegration of meaning as aspects of the subculture are picked up by main-stream fashion. Thus an item of clothing first made by art school students or worn by trendsetting musicians is soon copied by the fashion industry and marketed to young people all around the country. The fashion business and the commercial interests of the shops tend to soften the impact of particular styles. The manufactured version of a subcultural look has generally lost much of it original shock value. This process of adoption brings a gentler, less challenging, edge to the style making it more acceptable and less meaningful.

Hebdige's early understanding of youth culture is therefore somewhat élitist. The trendsetters are the true source of meaning. As the style spreads it becomes diluted and corrupted. Hebdige therefore sees the consuming of the average young person as lacking the real cutting edge of cultural criticism and creative energy which is seen in the art school world of the avant-garde. His work is to be seen in contrast to the work of people such as McRobbie who have emphasized the creative act which young women in particular engage in as they shop. In other words cultural creativity and meaning are open to all young people.

For subcultural theorists style has always been wider than how young people dress. In *Resistance through Rituals* Paul Corrigan described the behaviour of a group of young people in an essay called 'Doing Nothing'.[10] Corrigan investigated how groups of young people hanging around on the streets organized their time. His work uncovered the way that the group would gather in the same place waiting for something to happen. This behaviour was often mundane, but it held within it the possibility of excitement. Excitement might come when someone decides to kick a milk bottle around or when someone gets hold of a moped and drives round the precinct in an entertaining manner. Gangs of young people on the streets may appear unoccupied and somewhat threatening to the wider community, but Corrigan shows how a community relationship and activity is sustained for many young people when they are 'doing nothing'. A complementary picture of young people's lives is shown by Marsh, Rosser and Harré who studied the behaviour of groups of football supporters at Oxford United's football ground. The record of these studies, *The Rules of Disorder*, shows how the crowd is organized with different positions within the Oxford Road end.[11] The authors were able to observe by examining video-tape taken over a whole year that particular people stood in the same places in the stand every week. Some were younger boys on the fringe of things, others were 'the lads', others were older people who had once been where the action was, and others were the cheer-leaders who started the chants going. These positions in the stand indicated a definite hierarchy and career pattern for the football supporter. What might be seen as 'mob' behaviour tinged with anarchy according to *The Rules of Disorder*, is actually a well-organized social system based on commonly understood rules of behaviour. For those at the centre of 'disorder' there is actually order and community.

The British tradition of cultural studies represented by writers such as Hall, Brake, Hebdige and McRobbie has tended to locate meaning in popular culture within a struggle for identity between dominant culture and subcultures. This struggle might be variously understood as being based on social class, gender or race, however the key dynamic remains the same. Young people create a sense of self, community life and meaning by symbolic consumption and behaviour. They do this by the creative use of cultural artefacts delivered to them by the widespread availability of the products of mass production. The relationship between the industry of popular culture and the young people who consume the products of this industry forms the basis for the continuing discussion of popular culture.

Slaves to the Rhythm

The rise of popular culture has been seen by many Christians as a far from positive development. When dealing with youth culture and the role of the media, a Christian version of the culture industry argument has generally been adopted. According to this view the media carries within it a 'materialistic' message. The influence of advertising, television and pop music upon young people is viewed as being against the Christian gospel and thus a 'bad thing'. Popular music encourages hedonism, sexual promiscuity, idolatry and the occult. Christian young people should be warned of the dangers of listening to the wrong kind of music or watching the wrong kind of shows. According to the authors of *Dancing in the Dark*, modern media has found ways to market its products to what they call 'generational groups'.[12] The identification of separate age-related 'markets' for consumer products has meant that youth culture has been shaped by powerful economic forces. The culture industry has therefore created 'youth culture' to provide a willing and accessible group to whom dedicated products can be sold. The generation gap is a reality, but it is by no means an insurmountable problem, argues *Dancing in the Dark*. Indeed conflict between the young and the old is not a new phenomenon, being evident in ancient Greece and biblical time. What is new is that advertising and industry have in recent times sought to exploit these conflicts to sell into a designated and committed market. In this way separation between generations has been exaggerated to serve the ends of industry and multi-national corporations. Young people, according to this view, are therefore manipulated and duped by an all powerful media which holds all the cards.

The manipulative view of popular culture prevalent within Christian circles (especially in the United States) owes a good deal to the work of Neil Postman. Postman argues that technologies of communication impact upon the way that we discuss the world.[13] So the arrival of the telegraph in the United States brought about the culture of the news. The invention of the telegraph meant that communications between towns and countries became much quicker than the pace of a letter carried by horse or train. Suddenly it was possible to receive reports of events around the world almost instantaneously. Thus the news as we know it was born; but the telegraph not only increased the pace by which 'news' could be spread, it also packaged that news into short segments. The technology needed relatively short sentences and paragraphs which could be sent down the wires quickly and received with the minimum of misunderstanding. The news spoke of events from all over the country and eventually the world, but the seeming expansion of vision also brought a contraction of perspective. This contraction is imposed upon reality by the nature of the media used to convey the message. The selection and packaging of material to be sent as news inevitably affects the way that the world is viewed. A similar packaging can be seen as a result of the development of radio and television.

The process of cultural change led by technologies of communication has been a steady process of erosion. According to Postman television brings with it a reduction of rational discussion. On television the 'sound bite' has made political discussion into a short advert. How a politician looks is more important than what he or she says. The sound bite is more important than extended conversation on political matters. Image has triumphed over content and the reason for this is that television has become the chief arena for political discourse. The nature of the medium, argues Postman, is that it processes everything that it treats and homogenizes it into entertainment. In this way the distinctions between fact and fantasy are blurred. On television the assassination of a world leader, the latest video from a pop group and a soap opera all seem to look the same. Real-life tragedy and fictional disaster and technicolour advertising are all offered for our amusement. Entertainment not truth is the primary logic of television.

These kinds of insights have been seized on by Christians as evidence of moral corrosion associated with the media and popular culture. The role of Christian youthwork is to help young people to 'critique' what is presented to them by the media. According to John Buckeridge, Christians are to be particularly wary of advertising.[14] The millions spent by multinationals on researching youth culture is seen as good reason to warn young people that subtle and well-financed organizations are attempting to 'control' them. An all-out conspiracy theory is only just avoided but all the same 'youth culture' is viewed as being an arena which is full of dangers. This is well-illustrated by the way that magazines such as *Youthwork* run stories which tell of the 'occult' leanings of particular records or stars, or give alarming statistics of the use of drugs or the attitudes of pop singers.[15]

Inherent to these kinds of attitudes to the media is the view that young people are at risk and 'impressionable'. In contrast to the secular tradition of cultural studies, Christians have rarely attempted to value the culture which young people themselves create. Youth culture is more often seen in terms of a particular reading of the products which are offered to young people by the culture industry. Thus the media is regarded as powerful and dangerous. Young people themselves are seen as in need of instruction or even protection from the influence of advertising and youth culture. This kind of motivation can be seen in Christian campaigns against sexually explicit or violent videos or records. At the same time Christians have been very keen to develop their own alternative subculture for young people. This subculture has been created and maintained by Christian youthworkers.

Evangelical Christians have tended to be proactive in their use of modern technology and media to spread the gospel. Printing, radio, television, video, satellite, cable, the internet, in fact whatever new developments have come along, Christians have sought to use them 'for the kingdom'. Youthworkers have been right at the heart of these innovations. Youth ministry has been the means whereby the cultural forms associated with youth culture have been 'Christianized'. Thus we get Christian rap music and Christian dance music, etc. The intention behind these developments has been the creation of alternative Christian subcultures for young people. Through festivals, concerts, tapes and CDs young people are invited to consume the products of the Christian media industry. The problem with this approach is that it is still informed by an élitist 'culture industry' understanding of popular culture. Youth ministry has tended to focus attention on the content of the products of Christian media rather than on how young people use these products to create identity.

Christian commentators have generally adopted a negative view of popular culture. In some of the material developed within cultural studies a more positive view of meaning making and creativity from below has developed. A theological understanding of the Christian subculture will therefore need to focus not simply on the content and message of particular texts produced by Christian artists, it will also have to ask questions of how these texts are given meaning and significance by young people themselves. The key to this will be the development of a more sophisticated understanding of the relationship between cultural texts and the subcultures which young people create.

Identity and Popular Culture

In *Common Culture* Paul Willis examines the artistic life of young people. In contrast to art with a capital 'A', young people's lives, argues Willis, are to be seen as creative and imaginative. While most young people may well not be involved in the arts, their everyday lives are full of expressions, signs and symbols. These are used by individuals and groups to establish their 'presence' in society. The popular aesthetic of young people is used to build identity and meaning. This creative aspect of youth culture can be seen in the clothes that young people wear, in the way they do their hair, in the pictures which they use to decorate their bedrooms, in their use of slang, in the piercing and tattooing of their bodies, in the dances they create, and in the drama and ritual in their relationships.[16] Willis uses the concept of 'necessary work' to describe the importance of these symbolic modes of communication and association. Necessary work is that which we need to do in order to survive. For young people passing through adolescence means that they are in one way or another marginalized. The establishment of a sense of who they are in relation to others, says Willis, is a matter of survival and therefore necessary.[17]

Willis' view of youth culture is complemented by the work of John Fiske. Fiske argues that the culture industry fills its products with meanings, but these meanings will always need to find a resonance in people's lives.[18] The fact that films often fail is an indication that for all the investment in advertising and promotion, the media are not able to manipulate young people in the way that some critics and Christians suggest. Similarly in the record business the vast numbers of singles which are released each month in the UK should cause some pause for thought. Of the 700 or so released every week only a very small proportion ever find success. This means that the music industry is to a large extent at the mercy of the buying public. Popular culture therefore for Fiske resides in the way that groups of people create their own meanings from the products which they are offered. Mass culture which is manufactured and passed down to young people and others is largely a myth. Culture is a living thing which can only be developed from within, it cannot be imposed from above. The culture industry produces a repertoire of texts which groups of people use to create their own popular cultures.[19]

Willis uses the term 'common culture' for the process described by Fiske. Common culture refers to the necessary symbolic work of young people. Modern societies, according to Willis, are ones where traditional sources of meaning, belonging and security have been eroded. The concept of a 'whole' culture with defined places of meaning and understood roles and identities has long since passed. Organized religion, political affiliation, an identity supplied by location in the work place, schools and public broadcasting no longer offer commonly held values. In the past the passage from childhood to adulthood was well-defined and structured, but it has become more complicated and consequently less easy to travel. For young people marginalized from publicly understood sources of meaning, such things as the certainties of previous generations and of existing institutions which are merely living off the capital of the past, no longer remain plausible.[20] For those who might be seen as being on the edge of society, black young people or working-class women, these problems are particularly acute. The response has been the establishment of common cultures rooted in what Willis calls a 'grounded aesthetic', that is a sense that the culturally acceptable comes from young people themselves rather than from an artistic or indeed a religious establishment.[21] Common culture is seen in the way that young people and young adults are able to create 'proto-communities'.[22] These are informal communities which form around particular interests or events. Individuals may from time to time find themselves involved in a number of proto-communities. Proto-communities locate around a shared sense of style, a set of behaviours or an issue-based political group. An example of the latter would be the demonstrations against the bypass at Newbury. In these demonstrations a community of people was brought together which transcended the divisions usually associated with race, gender or social class. These kinds of proto-communities for a short while offer a sense of identity and purpose.

The Limitations of Cultural Studies

The work of people such as Fiske and Willis has encountered criticism from within the discipline of cultural studies. Jim McGuigan argues that what has emerged in recent times is an uncritical acceptance that significant meaning resides with the cultures created by groups of people. He calls this view 'cultural populism' in that it simply describes and celebrates popular culture.[23] The sense that cultural texts such as television might be read and critiqued in a literary manner has largely been abandoned in the face of the meanings which people make from television. The meaning of soap opera, for instance, has been presented as the way it offers particular 'pleasures' which derive from the way that the individual viewer reads the text, rather than the meaning which is located in the programme by industry or the script writer. Any confidence in a critical judgement as to the value or appropriateness of a particular cultural text has therefore tended to be left on one side. This lack of a critical perspective is largely the result of the collapse of a shared framework within which to assess the cultural value of texts. The confidence in a critique of culture has tended to be linked to the acceptance of an over-arching theory, such as high culture or the hegemonic struggle of different groups or the feminist interpretation of patriarchal structures of society.

For Christians engaged in working with young people the insights and the limitations of cultural studies are particularly informative. In the first place, the work of people such as Hall or McRobbie indicates that young people as they construct identities may well be doing so in reaction to problems of an economic or social nature. The Christian youthworker will want to first understand the signs and symbols of young people's style because these offer an insight into the social issues which concern groups of young people. If the gospel is to be good news for young people then it must be seen to encounter social as well as personal issues. The subculture created by young people therefore becomes the means by which the gospel can become meaningful within a particular subculture. This contextualizing will seek to express the faith within the language and style of the group, but it will at the same time develop a sensitivity to the underlying 'contradictions' from which the subculture has emerged.

It is for this reason that a Christian subculture as a safe retreat from the world that most young people live within is some-what problematic. To simply offer an alternative subculture to that which young people themselves have constructed is to miss the indications of how the gospel might be of more long-term relevance within communities. Youth culture indicates the areas where the power of God might start to be at work to bring about social change and transformation. Youth culture has highlighted issues concerning the environ-ment, it has led protests against war, and it expresses the lament of many young people out of work seeking a place in the world. It is in relation to these kinds of issues that Christian youthworkers can learn a good deal from the work of people such as Willis and Fiske. At the same time cultural studies indicates the importance that Christian young people have in the creation of a specifically Christian subculture within the Church. The assumption that Christian music is good and safe needs to be examined in the light of the work of cultural theorists such as Willis. Cultural studies points us away from the cultural texts and towards the culture which Christian young people themselves create. Our understanding of how the Christian subculture actually operates is at the present time fairly limited. We all swim in the pool, but we have never really analysed the water.

Cultural studies may well have lost a shared framework for critiquing culture, but Christians have not. The basis for our engagement in communities will remain the gospel. Andrew Walker refers to this as the 'grand narrative' of the Christian Church.[24] It is this narrative (summarized in Chapter 2) which gives us a critical perspective on popular culture. To say this, however, is somewhat different from the usual Christian approach to popular culture. Christian cultural analysis has tended to concentrate on youth culture as either a threat or as competition to the subculture offered by the Church. The rise of the Christian subculture has been generated by the feeling that a safe religious alternative to the harmful influence of popular youth culture should be offered to young people. The net result has been that the Church has regarded indigenous youth subcultures as 'competition'. Youth ministry has used the same methods as those which exist in the secular scene. Christian festivals compete in the same market-place as non-Christian festivals. Christian bands sell their products to young people in the same way as non-Christian artists. They each compete financially for young people's money and they compete for loyalty. Christian youth groups often feel that they are working in competition with the draw of sporting activities or other entertainments. Many youth ministers feel a sense of helplessness in the face of the increasing attractiveness of the popular media. There is also the possibility that those in the Church feel a sense of threat when young people adopt particular styles of dress. These attitudes come about not so much because of the demands of the gospel but because of the mind-set which arises from the attempt to compete in the market-place with popular culture. To engage missiologically with culture is somewhat different from attempting to establish a substitute culture which young people can buy into. The discipline of making the good news come alive within popular culture has a different trajectory from trying to tempt young people away from the culture which they themselves have adopted and created.

In the light of the gospel story Christian youthworkers should be looking for those aspects of popular culture which they can see as being in tune with the gospel while working for renewal and transformation of those aspects which are outside the parameters of God's intentions for society. Cultural studies therefore gives us tools to understand the culture of groups of young people, but it is the gospel which gives us a perspective to see these in a fresh light.

5

Youthwork and the Incarnation
of the Word

✳

THERE IS NO technique or method which guarantees results for
the Christian youthworker. However skilled and experienced
we may be, at the heart of our work is a mystery. This mystery
is based on the spiritual nature of what we are doing. What
makes Christian youthwork distinctive is the belief that
through our practice Jesus wishes to become real in young
people's lives. The presence of Jesus can be expressed in
terms of 'incarnation' – God taking flesh. Christian youthwork
is therefore a combination of our knowledge, skill, practice
and God's energy.

God's presence in our work and in the lives of the young
people we are meeting is not a right, it is a blessing. We cannot
expect that through our actions God will be present, neither
can we assume that a professional incompetence or lack of
skill as a youthworker might mean that God is not present.
The mystery of Christian youthwork is that 'the wind blows
where it wills'. We have no idea how the Holy Spirit is moving
in the lives of young people. The mission is God's, and therefore we are joining in with his activity not he with ours. In mission God is sovereign making his way where he wills. To
forget this is to make of our practice an idol. God becomes controlled by our programmes and expectations, and thus is no
God at all.

The 'spiritual' nature of Christian youthwork is not to be
expressed at the expense of human knowledge, expertise and
skill. To reach out with the gospel means that we must be
able to communicate effectively within the cultural world of
the young people we are meeting. The importance of the

work of God and our own efforts is expressed in an 'incarnational' theology of mission. This chapter examines the human side of mission amongst young people .

An incarnational theology of mission involves three kinds of journey, each of which requires particular skills and expertise. First, there is the journey which all adults need to make in order to communicate with young people. The youthworker needs to be willing and able to step outside the 'adult' way of relating and find a way to make contact within the natural environment of the teenager. This is a generational ① barrier. The second journey involves a movement from one subculture to another. The youthworker needs to be able to understand and communicate within the language patterns, social system and symbolic frameworks of a particular group. While some youthworkers may have grown up in an area and are therefore able to communicate 'naturally', for the majority the journey from one subculture to another has to take place. This is therefore a cultural barrier. The third journey involves the way that faith can be communicated from within one subculture to the subculture of another group. The first two journeys all youthworkers have in common, the third is unique to Christian youthwork. This chapter provides a basic framework to enable Christian youthworkers to understand how the faith becomes 'incarnated in culture'.

Aspects of the Incarnation of the Word in Culture

THE INCARNATION OF JESUS

The Christian faith rests on the belief that God became human in Jesus Christ. Jesus is 'the Word' become flesh; God's revelation within human history and human culture. When God chooses to communicate his message he does so using the language, customs and social relationships of a particular group of people in a particular time and in a particular place. Jesus was therefore a Jew born into a Jewish family. This means that the content of the 'good news' as we see it in the

Gospels is intimately connected to the social, political and spiritual context within which Jesus grew up and began to minister. This location of the Word of God within culture must be taken seriously by any Christian seeking guidance from the life of Christ. For while we may want to assert that God reveals himself in the life of Jesus, we must also acknowledge that this life was lived out in a time which was quite different from our own. The fact that the Word of God was incarnated within culture brings God closer to us, but it also creates a cultural distance for us.

Understanding the gospel story involves a process of thinking ourselves into the social world of the New Testament. We cannot read the Gospels directly into our present-day experience. The setting of the story colours not only the message of Christ, but also the way that good news takes shape in people's lives. The incarnation of Jesus forces the reader to deal with another culture and another time as the medium within which eternal truth is played out. Thus the cultural setting of the life of Christ forms an irreducible aspect of the story. This does not mean that we cannot understand the gospel or interpret it for today, nor does it mean that we have to be biblical scholars to get any kind of message from the text of scripture. It simply means that we have to work with the gospel text as a narrative which is located in a particular historical time.

The life of Christ is the revelation of God within culture. The location of the incarnation within a defined cultural setting means that we have no knowledge of God outside culture. To meet God through the story of Jesus in the New Testament is an experience within the culture, religious history and tradition of the Jews. God uses this culture to make himself known. A careful interpretation involves the reader in first thinking about the life-setting of the passage under consideration. This means not only the particular social and cultural situation of the passage, it also means viewing the passage in the light of a reading of the whole of the New Testament and the Old Testament. This kind of interpretative process arises directly from the means by which God has chosen to reveal himself.

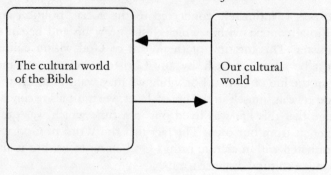

The Christian faith in the present era (or indeed at any time) is always an interpretation of the message. In each age the Church has the task of reading the Bible and making sense of it within its own social and cultural setting. The gospel which we have received and which has possibly changed our lives is still only one possible contextualization of the faith within culture. Culture is the medium within which faith is expressed and lived out. This insight does not mean that what we have received as the truth is in some way wrong. It simply means that we need to acknowledge the provisional nature of the faith as we understand it. The Church believes that it is the Holy Spirit who leads us into truth. It is the Spirit working within the body of believers who makes it possible to embrace our cultural expressions of the gospel as 'truth'. When Christians express the message of the gospel we do so within our own cultural frameworks.

The Christian faith must be expressed within culture for it to come alive for people. It is the task of the Church and of individual Christians to proclaim the message of Christ. Our proclamation however is not authoritative in itself. It is the revelation of Christ in the Bible which remains our sole authority. While we must seek to speak of God within our culture, our confidence in our own expression of the faith must be regarded as only one possible expression of the faith. When our theological deductions from the scriptures become confused with scripture itself we become idolatrous – we have substituted our words for the word of God. Such idolatry is particularly prevalent where the Church is so identified with

one particular culture that it has become culturally blind. It is
the experience of Christians within other cultural contexts
which alerts us to this kind of blindness. When we hear the
word of God which is true to the Bible and yet expressed within
another set of cultural norms we suddenly become aware of
our own cultural conditioning. For the youthworker an understanding of the cultural nature of the Christian faith is fundamental. Self-awareness is the basis for mission across cultures.
The first step to realizing that mission amongst young people
from outside the subculture of the Church is an understanding
of our own subcultural make-up. One way to achieve this is
to spend time with Christians from other parts of the world.
The experience of faith contextualized in other cultures helps
us to relativize our own understanding of the faith. This sets
us free to imagine the gospel expressed in new ways. In *Youth
Culture and the Gospel* I demonstrated this by showing a number
of pictures of Jesus drawn by Christians from around the
world.[1] The African picture showed a black Jesus, the Japanese
picture showed Jesus as an Oriental and, of course, the Western
Jesus was a white man. These different pictures give a clue as
to the way that faith can be expressed within culture. They
also point to our cultural bondage. This is particularly the
case where we find it hard to accept a picture of Jesus which is
different from our own. Youth ministers working across cultures and subcultures will need to develop an awareness of the
way that their own understanding of the Christian faith has
been shaped within a particular culture. This self-awareness is
the first step in contextualizing the gospel.

INCARNATION = BEING WITH

All youthwork is based on relationships with young people.
Christian youthwork is no different except that we see relationships not just as an end in themselves but as the means by
which young people may experience the presence of Christ.
The Christian youthworker is seeking to be a concrete expression of the Christian faith amongst a group of young
people. 'Being with' expresses this incarnational truth. To be
with young people is to get involved. There are Christian
approaches to youthwork which do not rely upon relationship.

An example would be the evangelist who arrives for a mission at a school one week and next week moves on to the next. This pattern of youthwork may have its place, but it is not incarnational, in that it lays very little, if any, emphasis upon the ongoing presence of the youthworker with a group of young people.

Incarnational youthwork as a method of outreach has much in common with the work of Christian missionaries. Missionaries such as Bible translators have evolved a long-term plan for the way that the gospel should be shared with groups of people who have not heard the message. In the first instance the Bible translator will prepare by developing a full acquaintance with the Bible in its original languages. This preparation will take a long time and much study; however, this is only half the picture. Academic study of the Bible is only a preparation, because the task is to translate the text from the original languages into the thought forms and language of the new group of people. Having studied the Bible the translator must then get to know the culture of the people with whom he or she wishes to share the message. This means going and living with the people over a long period of time so that the structure, grammar and the vocabulary of the language can be learned. There will also be a need to understand the ritual and symbolic language of the community. There is again no short cut to this. The translator must be so involved in the life of the people that through observation and conversations with the people a true understanding of the community can begin to develop. In some situations the translator has had to create a written form of a language that has so far only ever been spoken. This is necessary before it is possible to translate the biblical text into that language. When it comes to translating, the missionary will ideally not be seeking a literal expression of the biblical text, the message will need to be contextualized. This is done by what Charles Kraft calls 'dynamic equivalents' in translation, e.g. in communities where sheep do not exist other animals might be used to translate the image of Jesus as the Lamb of God.[2] By such means a presentation of the biblical message can emerge which is true to the original text, but which also makes sense in the culture of the people.

For Christian youthwork 'being with' must precede any verbal expression of the faith. Like the translator of the Bible the youth minister is also in a missionary situation of moving from one cultural setting to another. Our first task is to learn the language, social behaviour, values and symbolic expressions of the young people we are working with. The only way that we can do this is to spend time in regular informal contact with the young people we want to reach. Informal time means that we are not running a programme or a meeting. It means that we are in contact with the group when they are relating naturally. When we are in charge of a meeting young people tend to conform to our ways of speaking and relating. When we are doing contact work with them, they relate in ways which are more indigenous to them. It is only when we are being with a group as they relate normally that we are able to understand and communicate within their particular subculture.

The time we spend in informal contact with young people forms the basic resource for our verbal proclamation of the gospel. If we cut short informal time, or if we dispense with it altogether, we have no guarantee that what we are doing is a contextualization of the faith. The likelihood is that as we share the faith we impose our own culture at the same time. Just like the missionaries who exported English church architecture, music and worship to Africa and India, we are resorting to the same kind of cultural imperialism. Being with young people gives us the ability to see the gospel through their eyes so that when we come to 'translate' the message for them, we do so out of a respect and intimacy with their own subculture and social context.

Being with, however, is itself an expression of the gospel. As we spend time with young people we find that we are a reflection of the love of God amongst them. The respect which we show as we spend time getting to know groups and individuals is a witness to the presence of Christ amongst the group. The way that we go about outreach amongst young people is therefore a sign of the gospel. We are the means by which Jesus becomes incarnated amongst a group of young people. To be 'incarnational' as a youthworker is therefore to live out a spirituality which is deeply rooted in the life of Christ. We are imitators of Christ attempting, by the things which we do and say, to offer young people an insight into the heart which God has for them. Our concern is a powerful sign of God's regard for young people. The things which we disapprove of similarly indicate the priorities of the kingdom of God. An incarnational approach to youthwork would hold that the way we share the gospel is as much a sign of the good news as what we say. By implication it would distance itself from methods of evangelism which seem to violate this principle.

THE WORD IN TRANSLATION

Translation of the gospel rotates around three poles. The Bible, the culture of the translator, and the culture of the people for whom the translation is being made.

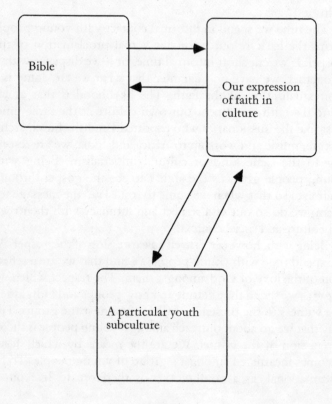

Sharing the faith from one culture to another or from one subculture to another is based upon the interaction of these three poles. First the youthworker needs to have a good grasp of the biblical material. This is a part of youthwork training which can sometimes be missed. In particular we can be guilty of a favourite passage or proof text approach to reading the scriptures. Youthworkers are often activists and reluctant to spend long periods of time reading material which does not immediately impact our work, even if what they are reading is the Bible. Being with young people often seems more attractive than academic study. The current enthusiasm for worship can also erode our familiarity with the Bible. For some youthworkers brought up on charismatic worship, a commitment to the study of the Bible can seem a little tame. These tendencies have weakened their ability to translate the message to young people who are outside the social groups which currently make up the Church.

We need to read the whole of the Bible to have a firm grasp on the gospel story. If we keep to well-trodden paths or rely upon the immediacy of the Spirit in worship, our problem is that we have not allowed the Bible to call our assumptions about the faith into question. Karl Barth entitled one of his early essays 'The Strange New World Within the Bible'.[3] The youthworker needs to spend time exploring the depth and variety of this strange, new world of the Bible. Regular in-depth Bible study, which takes us into the less well-known parts of the text, introduces us to people whose experience of God was very different from our own. In the strange new world of the Bible we find that the nice, caring 'Father' of our choruses and church worship seems to engage in a good deal of judgement and bloodshed. Moreover in the Bible we discover that people whom we would never put into leadership in our groups seem to be used by God to bring about his heavenly purposes. When we move away from the familiar territory of scripture into less well-known areas, we are surprised by the sheer variety of ways of talking about God, praying and worshipping that we find expressed in the Bible.

Entering the strange new world of the Bible gives us a clue that the Christian faith as we have been taught it is conditioned by culture. The rich diversity of spiritual experience and expression in the biblical material gives us an indication that our own faith, though very helpful and relevant, may not be the only possible way of living out the Christian faith. This sense of 'relativity' concerning the tradition which we have inherited is essential to successful translation. Without the possibility that the Christian faith might look and sound different, the translator will tend to replicate what he or she feels most familiar with. The Bible is therefore not only the source for the gospel message, it is also the means by which we are able to imagine this message expressed differently.

An intimate knowledge of culture is also required to share the Christian faith with young people. This sensitivity only comes from time spent with groups and individuals. Translation happens when the youthworker begins to look through the eyes of young people's culture at the Bible. This again is largely a matter of imagination and trial and error. Looking through their eyes means that we bring the life experiences, questions and values of the group to the biblical material. Translation also means looking from the Bible to the young people's lives and from young people's lives to the Bible. The question which the youthworker has to keep in the forefront of his or her mind is 'What is the good news for this group?'

What is good news depends upon which aspect of the gospel story brings God's life to young people. It is this good news which must be proclaimed. The youthworker is the means by which young people initially hear the translated message. The translation of the message is not an academic exercise, it is essentially practical. In the first instance it affects the way youthwork is carried out in practice (for more on this see Chapter 6). How we do youthwork should be shaped by what we think is good news for the young people we are working with. Christian youthwork can be very diverse, for instance it can focus on the offer of support or it can primarily concern itself with challenge, it can be mainly spiritual or it can have an emphasis upon social concern, it can be based in a locality or it can bring young people together from around the world. Each of these possibilities (and of course there are a good many more) might be good news to different groups of young people. It is the job of translation to make the right choice of style of youthwork practice. A major criticism of Christian youthwork is that it very rarely shapes its practice around a concern to be good news amongst a particular group of young people. More often than not the style of a youthwork project arises because it is perceived to be successful elsewhere. Youthwork in this way spreads by one group copying another. An incarnational approach to youthwork will put a high priority on shaping the work around a faithfulness to the Bible and a sensitivity to the subculture of a particular group of young people. Ideas gleaned from elsewhere should be judged in the light of this.

Christian youthworkers are called to proclaim the gospel in both word and deed. Telling the gospel message to a group of unchurched young people can be very challenging. Most youthworkers feel a certain anxiety when they come to talk about the Christian faith for the first time. Some of this anxiety comes because in past experience most of us have seen young people respond negatively to an overt preaching of the gospel. These negative experiences, however, generally come about where Christians have tried to preach the gospel to young people they don't know or in situations which the young people feel that the message is inappropriate. The challenge for incarnational youthworkers is to use their close knowledge of the culture of the young people to overcome these problems.

In the first instance the successful translator of the gospel will be the person who finds a situation where the young people themselves are open to hearing the message. This means that the group will need to feel that they are consulted about the introduction of stories about Jesus. It could be that the best approach to this is for the youthworker to make storytelling a normal part of her contact work with the group. Telling the gospel story then becomes a steady and natural part of the life of the group. The key, however, in doing this lies in finding a way of telling the story which does not seem forced or out of order to the group.

Having found the right situation, the next stage involves the decision as to what is best said. In many situations the young people will have no knowledge of the Bible or the Christian faith. The responsibility is therefore for the youthworker to choose the right kind of message based on the Bible which will make sense in the young people's lives. Inspiration for this process can be drawn from published interpretations of the Bible such as Eugene Petersen's *The Message* and Walter Wangerin's *The Book of God* [4] In most cases it is inappropriate to simply lift passages from such books. Both Wangerin and Petersen, while being very talented, are conditioned by their own cultural setting. What works for North Americans or even what works in our church setting may not be the best translation for groups of young people in Britain. The best approach is for the youthworker to use these versions of the Bible as a guide and an inspiration. Reading a passage in *The Message* or *The Book of God* can give the youthworker a new angle on a biblical passage and begin to spark new thoughts for a dynamic translation which is rooted in the experience and lives of particular groups of young people.

THE INCARNATION OF THE WORD IN THE LIVES OF YOUNG PEOPLE

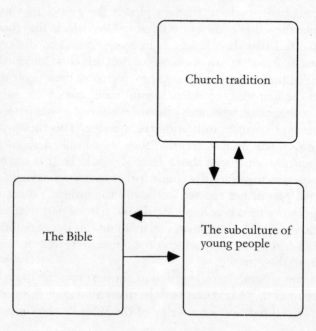

The eventual aim of youth ministry should be that young people begin to develop the faith within their own cultural world. When young people hear and respond to the message which is translated into their world through the words and actions of youthworkers and other members of the Church, a new situation arises. The young person who has newly come to faith is able to access the Bible for himself. The hope is that he does this while remaining within his own subculture. For some young people reading the Bible will be a distinct possibility, especially if they are introduced to one of the more readable modern translations. My own current favourite is the Common English Version which is produced in this country by the Bible Society. The advantage of this text, which was first designed to be read out loud, is that it follows the rhythms of modern speech. This means that it tends to make sense to the everyday reader on first sight. It also has the advantage of keeping to a relatively simple vocabulary. For a good many other young people reading may not be the best way of accessing the biblical material. The youthworker in this situation will need to continue as storyteller. This can be substituted by using videos which portray the gospel in drama. The *Jesus of Nazareth* series is a good resource in this respect.

However the biblical material is put into the hands of the young people, the role of the youthworker is to act as a guide to the group. Space for discussion and for prayer means that young people can begin to process the stories from the Bible into practical Christian discipleship within their own context. The hope is that what develops is an approach to being Christian and to believing which is indigenous to the subculture of the young people. As more young people begin to join in with this process, a new Christian community starts to emerge. (How this community begins to find a worshipping life of its own is explored in more depth in Chapter 7.)

The Limitations of Contextualization

There are dangers in any contextualization of the gospel. The desire is that the Christian faith is incarnated within the subculture of a group of young people; unfortunately it is possible for this process to go astray. It is a major temptation to so accommodate the gospel to the culture of the group that essential aspects of the Christian message become blunted. For instance the desire to make the gospel attractive may play down the demand for personal or social morality. Dietrich Bonhoeffer warned the Church of the dangers of cheap grace, that is the offer of God's blessing and acceptance without the demands of following Christ. Bonhoeffer's message in *The Cost of Discipleship* sounds a note of warning to youthworkers today, just as it did to the German Church in the 1930s.[5] The story of the co-operation of the Church with a pagan and even occult Nazi state in Germany is a salutary warning for any contextualization today.

Young people seeking a path of Christian discipleship need to hear the voices of others within the Christian tradition to keep them on track. In the first instance it is the task of the youthworker, and other mature Christians involved with the group, to bring into the creative contextualizing process the wisdom which is there in the history and tradition of the Church. The road to working out the faith in a new cultural setting is lined with blind alleys – to believe otherwise is to fly in the face of the history of the Church. There is no reason to believe that a group of young people are not immune to the temptation of accommodating the gospel to their culture, making a tame replica of the God of the Bible who affirms everything which they think and do. This kind of comfortable accommodation has been a feature of church history and indeed of present-day church culture. Young people need the insights which come from the history of the wider Church to bring a sense of balance and maturity to their pilgrimage. True contextualization requires a rootedness in culture, a faithfulness to the Bible, and an openness to the tradition of the Church.

6

Getting Started: Two Case Studies

EVANGELICALS HAVE TENDED to think of the gospel as a series of propositions. Each proposition leads logically on to the next. Thus an evangelistic presentation will consist of a series of statements. To lead someone to Christ involves a process of moving them through this sequence. A simple summary of the gospel might read like this:

1. We are fallen and sinful and therefore separated from God.
2. Jesus died for our sins on the cross to bring us back to God.
3. To be reunited with God we must ask for forgiveness of our sins, accept that Jesus died for us, and receive his forgiveness.

It is possible to critique this kind of presentation. One way would be to indicate that the presentation of the gospel in these statements is incomplete in some way. Some would, for instance, be keen to start the explanation of the gospel with a statement that gives prominence to God's love for humanity as part of creation. This would be expressed as a theological argument, i.e. that the gospel story places a prior emphasis upon creation rather than the fall. This may or may not be the case but what we should also bear in mind is that the first proposition in a linear understanding of the gospel will tend to determine how we relate to people whom we are seeking to introduce to the faith. The starting point of a linear understanding of the gospel is therefore a kind of doorway through which we hope people will pass as they become Christians. If we see the entry point to the linear sequence as human sinfulness, then we will be wanting to 'convict' people of sin. If, however, we see the starting point as the love of God, then we will tend to find ways to express this insight by being warm and accepting. For the youthworker seeking to contextualize the gospel in the lives of young people, the linear model of presenting the message has significant problems.

Linear summaries of the gospel tend to simplify biblical narrative. In the three-point outline above, for instance, the meaning of Christ's death on the cross has been expressed solely in terms of a sacrifice for sin. In contrast it is possible to see in the biblical material and in the tradition of the Church a number of different understandings of the death of Christ.[1] Christians have at different times responded to Christ's death as a victory over death or evil, others have been moved by the self-giving of Christ to follow a new way of life, and more recently the suffering of Christ has been expounded as an identification with the suffering of humanity. The gospel is a complex story which carries within it a number of different and complementary meanings. The summary I have presented above is not necessarily wrong, it is just one possible route of interpretation through the gospel narrative. For those involved in communicating the faith to young people, a simple presentation of the gospel has always been attractive. The problem is that reliance upon one expression of the message reduces the number of available interpretations.

Sharing the faith across cultures and subcultures requires us to keep an open mind therefore on two characteristics of the gospel. First, we need to see that there are many possible doorways into the faith. Second, there are a number of legitimate interpretations of key moments in the gospel narrative, such as the cross of Christ, or the nature and effect of human sinfulness. These two considerations mean that a reductive linear construction of theological propositions is severely limiting for Christian youthwork. A more helpful understanding of the gospel might be to see theological truth as a 3D honeycomb or cluster of ideas. Any one of the key ideas within the honeycomb can act as an entry point or doorway. Instead of a linear progression of the gospel narrative with a prescribed order for understanding the message, a honeycomb approach would see understanding as developing in a more organic way – one cell of the honeycomb to the other. Full Christian discipleship only comes when all of the key cells in the honeycomb are understood and incorporated into the lives and culture of the young people who are coming to faith.

This concept of the gospel allows for the fact youthworkers will want to live out the gospel amongst young people in a variety of different ways depending upon the subculture which they are working within. This understanding of the faith also means that in speaking about the gospel, the youthworker can start with the part of the honeycomb which is most appropriate to the context of the group. At the same time the honeycomb will act as a reminder that the Christian faith must be encountered as a network of truths and interpretations of the gospel.

Andrew Walker's description of the gospel as the 'grand narrative of the Christian people' complements the honeycomb idea. Walker describes evangelism as the process by which the gospel comes alive for us as we begin to see our own lives caught up in the grand story of God.[2] Stories engage different people in different ways. We are caught up in the narrative when we begin to identify with particular moments within the story. In other words there are different parts of the story which ring true for different groups of people, different cultures or subcultures. The narrative pattern of the gospel, however, demands that for a complete understanding of the story of God, and indeed of ourselves, we need to ultimately engage with the full flow of the story. To be part of God's story we need the whole plot, but we can get in touch with the story by starting at a number of different points. So eventually the entire honeycomb needs to be explored; or to put it another way, the whole of the narrative needs to become a place of identity and meaning for those coming to faith. The key factor in how this comes about will be finding the right starting point in the honeycomb or in the story. It is the starting point which locates the practice of youthwork within the gospel story (or places it within the honeycomb). Christian youthwork which is committed to the gospel must be shaped by an appreciation of the importance of this starting point.

This chapter presents two case studies. The case studies describe the social situation of two different groups of young people who live in the same town. First, the social world of the group is described. The gospel is then looked at to see what a possible starting point for a contextual mission might be with this group. Finally, in the light of the social context of the group and the chosen starting point within the gospel story, an approach to youth ministry amongst the group is set out. These case studies are fictional constructions. However, they are based upon the work of successive groups of students at Oxford Youth Works who each year study real groups of young people and follow a similar pattern of contextual theologizing.

Case Study 1

This group of working-class fourteen-year-olds have all grown up on a predominately working-class estate. Their parents are variously in and out of work. Mostly their work has been some kind of manual labour. A number of the boys come from fairly disrupted families and in one or two cases only one parent is currently at home. The group all attend the local comprehensive school, but they are not amongst the most academically successful. They expect to leave school with very few qualifications and they know that means jobs will be hard to come by.

The boys all dress similarly. They wear what is considered 'mainstream' clothes at their school – baggy jeans and baggy cotton tops. They usually wear large trainers with bouncy air filled soles. Particular attention is paid to the make of their shoes and at this moment in time they favour Nike. The group wear baseball caps high on their head, the right way round. The logo on the front of the caps in most cases reads, 'Chicago Bulls'. All the group speak with a marked local accent. The individuals in the group are not particularly communicative; however, they will talk at some length about the latest exploits of the joy-riders. While not in the main league in taking cars and displaying them on the estate, some of the group have been involved in this illegal activity. One of the lads has already been arrested for car crime and his case is due to be heard in a few months' time.

Trouble seems a feature of many of the lives of those in the group. One reason for this is their attitude. They all share an anti-authoritarian stance when it comes to the police, school and even some of their parents. They get into trouble fairly regularly but confrontation with authority is not seen as an end in itself by the group. They regard trouble with the police or with the school as a natural, and possibly unfortunate, consequence of the activities they choose to indulge in. The group shares a tight friendship with each other based on shared activities and possibly arising from the reaction they inspire in others. They have an acute sense of group loyalty. The unforgivable sin is to 'grass up a mate'. Despite their closeness and their illegal activities each of the individuals shows signs of a lack of self-esteem. The friendship of the group goes some way to compensating for this.

GOOD NEWS FOR THE GROUP

The Gospels show Jesus taking particular notice of those who were on the underside of his society. The good news is to be proclaimed to the 'poor' (Luke 4.18). Jesus seems to have made a particular point of eating and socializing with those groups who were disadvantaged or who lacked choices. At one point Jesus is questioned about the company he keeps:

> And the Pharisees and their scribes murmured against his disciples, saying, 'Why do you eat and drink with tax collectors and sinners?' And Jesus answered them, 'Those who are well have no need of a physician, but those who are sick; I have not come to call the righteous, but sinners to repentance.' (Luke 5.30-2)

Those regarded as sinners were the people who, for one reason or another, were unable to keep the complex web of purity laws followed by the Pharisees. Joachim Jeremias calls these the 'people of the land' – the ones who worked for a living but whose work kept them out of synagogue life.[3] For instance those working with animals would of necessity come into contact on a daily basis with animal dung, or other material. Under Jewish purity laws this would make them ritually unclean and excluded them from worship. The people of the land therefore were those who were outside the acceptable world of Jewish religious life, and yet Jesus built relationships with them. Edward Schillebeeckx sees the 'table fellowship' of Christ as a portent of God's coming kingdom. By eating and drinking with sinners Jesus brings the possibility of new life and signals freedom.[4] The kingdom of God is a great feast where in the absence of the invited guests the roads are searched for those who are hanging around. Both the good and the bad enter in (Matthew 22.1–10).

In the Gospels we see Jesus developing a particular relationship with the people of the land. Like the young people in the case study, they lived on the margins of acceptable behaviour – sometimes inside the law and sometimes outside it. Jesus is clear that they are sinners and that they need the healing work of the doctor, but he appears to be willing to compromise his religious identity and respectability in order to bring the kingdom to them. Moreover, while repentance and new life are seen to come from these encounters what evidence we have of this seems to confound the expectations of the religious community.

It is the presence of Christ amongst the people of the land which brings about change and renewal. Tax collectors, prostitutes and political rebels are all turned around by relationship with Jesus. These people were seen as lacking in social worth by the religious people of the day. In contrast Jesus offers the high honour of sharing meal-times and he invites them to join his fellowship of followers. These people may well have been outside the synagogue, but they had a place in the kingdom which Jesus came to proclaim. There are moments when the warmth of relationship and encounter between Jesus and the people of the land are a disturbing sign of the coming kingdom. An example of this is where Jesus is dining with a Pharisee and a prostitute gatecrashes the evening and starts to weep at Jesus' feet washing the tears away with her hair (Luke 7.36–50). The intimacy of this encounter is a powerful sign of the coming kingdom and a rebuke to the Pharisee, as Jesus later points out:

> 'Do you see this woman? I entered your house, you gave me no water for my feet, but she has wet my feet with her tears and wiped them with her hair. You gave me no kiss, but from the time I came in she has not ceased to kiss my feet. You did not anoint my head with oil, but she has anointed my feet with ointment.' (Luke 7.44–6)

The behaviour of the woman in the society of the day was outrageous. Any respectable religious person would have been incensed. It is possible that despite this the Pharisee in the story is embarrassed into inaction by the effrontery of the woman. She is a righteous rebel in that her faithfulness calls the Pharisee's religious commitment into question.

THE WAY IN FOR YOUTHWORK

In the Gospels we see Jesus making a point of spending time with the people of the land. Incarnational youthwork would see the importance of this kind of contact ministry, not simply as a technique of reaching out to young people – contact work for this group is the key method of sharing the good news. The lack of self-worth and the compensatory behaviour and identity of the group mean that the youthworker must also identify strongly with the young people. The example of sharing meals seen in the Gospel record of the life of Jesus can be paralleled by the many occasions where the group 'hangs out' on the street corner. Identification with the group will not involve approval of joy-riding or any other illegal activity, but it might tolerate the skill, energy and organization involved in stealing and displaying a car. The enthusiasm for motor sport might be a starting point for extended contact with the group. The priority, however, will be to make sure that these young people experience the love of God through the ongoing presence of the youthworker in the life of the group.

When it comes to sharing the gospel story a major priority should be placed on presenting Jesus as a working man who identified with those who were similar in class and background to himself. This Jesus is one who spoke with the accent of his region, who had time for the outsider, who was not soft on wrongdoing, but who always made space to spend time with his friends down the pub. The distant Church which speaks with a middle-class accent needs to be corrected by a vision of Jesus who identified with a local community. The love of God seen in the caring work of the youthworker and in the story of the gospel needs to be the recurring theme of proclamation. The young lads need to feel that God values them and that he is very much concerned with what they want to do with their lives. God is on their side.

The loyalty of the group offers a sign of the kingdom of God. Jesus also had a group of closely linked mates. They went off on jaunts together, just like the group does. The disciples where Jesus' special friends who shared his mission and his lifestyle. Jesus was the kind of person who was there for his friends when times were tough. But he was not the kind of friend who didn't let you know what the score was. Jesus was straightforward and honest and if the disciples were out of order, then he let them know it. The difference for Jesus and the disciples is that they were involved in living for God's kingdom. This is qualitatively different from the lads' activities of taking cars or stealing for fun. The disciples' identity was based on their relationship to Jesus, not their feelings at that time. This kind of connection needs to be made for the young people to respond to the love of God.

Following Christ should also be linked to the clear need for these young men to find jobs. Jobs give not only money, but also identity and self-worth. To be earning is to have made it. Youthwork must not be a distraction from this process. Our understanding of discipleship must have an immediate pay-off for the lads in terms of helping them to move into work. This might mean supporting members of the group as they go through a course at the College of Further Education; it might mean that every week the group prays for aspects of training and applying for work. The youth minister may go further and set up a scheme to employ the lads, this could possibly be linked to working on cars. In all of this, faith in Christ and moving on in life need to be explicitly linked.

Faith in Christ does not mean fitting into a Christian middle-class stereotype. It is possible to be outrageous to religious people in the way we worship God and express our relationship with him. The group need to see that Jesus wants them to be natural in their fellowship and in their church life. This might, for instance, mean that when they pray they occasionally use swear words or at the worship time they allow smoking, or that they only invite working-class people to speak at the worship. All of these would be fairly shocking within a church setting, but for this group they may be an aspect of contextual-ization within culture which is simply natural – as well as being outrageous. Like the woman who washed Jesus' feet with her tears, these young people will be trying to be Christians the best way they can. Their actions may cause offence, but that is just part of their faithfulness to Christ.

Case Study 2

This group of ten young people come from a more leafy part of the town. About a third of the catchment area of the school is made up of privately owned three- and four-bedroomed houses. The young people in the group all live in this type of house. In all but one case the young people live with both their natural parents. The parents of the group all work in middle-class or professional occupations, e.g. lecturers, solicitors, nurses or middle managers.

The group are seen by themselves and by the other staff and pupils in the school as the successful 'in crowd'. They generally occupy the central table in the school coffee lounge most lunch-times. They are noisy and full of jokes. Being around them is fun. They are attractive, open and welcoming, but also a little intimidating for the outsider to join. They all expect to do well at school and to go on to university. Their eventual aims include working in the media, running their own busi-nesses and being sports physiotherapists. In general the ambi-tions of the group are towards high-profile, well-paid jobs which offer a challenging and interesting life. They are aiming for success and they are expected to achieve it. Pressure to succeed comes not only from their homes, but also from the school. The teachers are aware that the A level results, and therefore league table ranking of the school, rest largely in the hands of this group.

All the group work on Saturdays and on occasional evenings. They are therefore extremely busy, but on Saturday night they party. All of them have false IDs to get into the town centre pubs where they drink large amounts and 'get wrecked'. This is their way of letting off steam. They are also fairly regular drug users, smoking cannabis at the weekends. Their parents and the school are basically aware of what the group gets up to. The agreement, however, is that if they get their schoolwork done and they continue to do well, then what they do every now and again is their own business.

The conversation within the group is extremely superficial, rarely moving out of joking and larking around. The group has no sense of any real problems in life. If there are problems they all feel able to talk with their parents and at school they find the staff to be approachable and helpful.

THE GOOD NEWS FOR THE GROUP

The doorway to the gospel for this group cannot be based upon any sense of need, or indeed, sinfulness. The loving, caring presence of a youthworker may well be welcomed, but any depth of relationship might prove very difficult. The group are so secure in their successful path through school and on into adult life that they have little need of another adult person with whom to share their troubles. Contact work alone therefore will leave the youthworker with a good deal of fun interaction with the group, but very little progress. The youthworker who sees him or herself as someone offering care in answer to need will find that there is no way into the gospel honeycomb for this group. A more appropriate expression of the gospel might start with a commitment to challenge the priorities of the group.

The Parable of the Talents represents the kingdom of God as being related to the responsible and entrepreneurial use of gifts and abilities to bring about economic success (Matthew

25.14–30). The servants in the story are given differing amounts of money according to their abilities. When the master returns they are called to account for what they have done with this money and they are rewarded for making a hefty profit. The message is that the kingdom of God is related to the responsible use of God-given prosperity and opportunity. Those who are given a great deal are expected to produce a great deal. Prosperity in itself, however, is not really the goal. The story of the rich man who tore down his barns to build bigger ones strikes a warning note.

> And he said, 'I will do this: I will pull down my barns, and build larger ones; and there I will store all my grain and my goods. And I will say to my soul, Soul you have ample goods laid up for many years; take your ease, eat, drink, be merry.' But God said to him, 'Fool! This night your soul is required of you; and the things you have prepared, whose will they be?' So is he who lays up treasure for himself, and is not rich toward God. (Luke 12.8–21)

Making it in the kingdom involves working for God. This means using the gifts and abilities which he has given us to achieve great things for him, not necessarily for our own pleasure or enjoyment. The call of the disciples gives another clue to this (Mark 1.14–20). The disciples were asked by Jesus to 'Follow me', this meant a costly turning away from their previous life and entering another much more challenging one. Jesus asks every Christian to make a difference in the world, but those who have much are expected to give the most.

Tony Campolo has developed an approach to youthwork in a North American context where many Christian young people are privileged and wealthy. He points out that young people are turned on by challenge. It is in this way, he says, that evangelistic organizations have inspired thousands of young people to set out to try to 'convert the world for Christ'. A seemingly otherworldly invitation to reach beyond ourselves is very attractive. To be an entrepreneur for the kingdom of God brings out heroism amongst young people. Campolo sees that there is much to be learned from the idea of a holy crusade and many young people are yearning for a way to make a mark in the world. To do this at the invitation of God and in his name is a radical and dynamic lifestyle choice for young people and one which is very attractive.[5]

The call to follow Christ therefore should start with the challenge to live a different life. The focus for this group should not be on the needs of the young people whether these be seen as social or spiritual. These young people are winners wanting to make their mark in life. They want to be creative and business-like. The key message is that these things of themselves are God-given desires and talents. The question is to what ends are they going to give their lives? The youthworker needs to devise a strategy to offer radical new options to the group for heroic service in the cause of the kingdom of God. These young people are ambitious; the task of the youthworker is to show how God wants them to use their talents positively for him.

Repentance therefore takes the form of challenging the group to choose a new kind of lifestyle. This does not mean an undue attention on the recreational use of alcohol or drugs, however wrong this might be. The starting point must be the presentation of other attractive options for giving their lives in the service of God and other people. One option could be to introduce the group to Christians who are running their own businesses. Work experience schemes give the chance for young people in their later years at school to spend time with companies and businesses. A placement with Christians running or working in a media or publicity company might offer an insight into a creative use of energy which operates within a Christian framework. The role of the youthworker is not just to set up this kind of opportunity, but also to spend time with individuals talking through what they have experienced. The gospel implications of what the young people are experiencing can then be unpacked and worked through. How Christ meets the challenge to achieve something in life can become an overt part of the discussion.

Another approach might be to take the group on a trip abroad to see how Christian charities are working with people in the Two-Thirds World through projects such as an income generation scheme. This kind of small investment use of capital to stimulate business amongst groups of poor people to whom the banks have been reluctant to lend can offer an inspiring example of how the young people themselves can make a difference by using their own gifts and skills. The Christian context of these kinds of charitable initiatives offer the occasion for the youthworker to speak of Jesus as someone who calls us to follow him by giving our lives in similar efforts to make the world a better place. Campolo has devised schemes whereby relatively wealthy young people spend time working alongside Christians who are caring for the poor. The example of self-giving lives which are filled with prayer and spiritual energy in the face of quite awful suffering raises questions in the minds of young people. According to Campolo this kind of challenge to service in the kingdom evangelizes young people in ways that the traditional understanding of the gospel rarely touches.[6]

These case studies offer an insight into the way that specific youthwork projects can be fundamentally shaped by both the call of the gospel and the social context of young people.[7] The process of getting close to a group and reading the gospel through their eyes offers an insight into the way that missiological strategies for translating the gospel can reshape the way youthwork is done. This approach can be adopted both for work outside-in and for work which is inside-out. The second case study has particular relevance for more privileged Church young people who may have grown somewhat complacent about the faith.

7

Youth Church:
Meaning Making and Worship

WORSHIP IS THE goal of Christian youthwork. The only adequate response to the gospel is to worship God. Christian youthwork will therefore include within its activities occasions where young people can experience worship and where they can start to worship for themselves. A commitment to the contextualization of the gospel means that new forms of worship will start to emerge. How this new community of believers relate to the existing Church is a major issue for youthwork. Negotiating with the institution of the Church is only one of the problems to be faced when starting a new congregation or youth church. Basic to contextualization is the ability to create something which is meaningful and new. This chapter starts by looking at the relationship between the Church and youth churches or congregations. The second part of the chapter examines the way that worship creates meaning for young people and how creativity can be encouraged.

Youth Church

The present youthwork scene is characterized by considerable discussion concerning youth congregations or youth churches. On the one hand, some clergy and youthworkers are concerned to preserve the 'family' feel of the local congregation. It is argued that the Church is where people of all ages and types gather together to worship God. Fragmentation into different 'congregations' or churches flies in the face of the biblical emphasis upon the power of the gospel to bring people together. On the other hand, there are an increasing number of people within the youthwork world who are actively setting up churches which are based solely on one age group. One example of this would be the creation of a student church as an alternative to a university Christian Union. Some people would argue that the typical Christian Union or youth group is just an artificial construction – a club. The true means to evangelize and nurture people in the faith is the Church and the best type of church to reach students is one which is contextualized within their culture.

This debate has the potential to be extremely heated, I realize. I find myself to be in sympathy with both sides of the argument. I can see that the unity of the Church is a gospel imperative. The 'oneness' of the believers is a witness to the oneness of God. The message of Paul to the Galatians should cause us to reflect upon the increasing divisions in the Church:

> For as many of you as were baptized into Christ have put on Christ. There is neither Jew nor Greek, there is neither slave nor free, there is neither male nor female; for you are all one in Christ Jesus. (Galatians 3.27–8)

At the same time there have always been churches and groups within churches which reflect different cultures and emphases. In the earliest times such a divide was evident between Gentile and Jewish communities as can be seen in the discussions between Paul and the Jerusalem church in Galatians 2. The Church therefore lives with a tension between cultural diversity and the unity which we have in Christ. For the youth minister this question of unity and cultural diversity has become particularly important. It is my view that much of the current discussion concerning youth churches and new forms of worship can be resolved by an examination of what we mean by the term 'church'.

The Church as Missionary Project, Community Group and Institution

The word 'church' carries a number of different meanings. For many people church is simply a building, for others it is a reference to the people who meet in that building. Church can be used for a national organization or a denomination, but it also can be used to speak of the ecumenical unity of all Christians everywhere – the universal Church. Church also has a spiritual connotation as in 'the body of Christ'. In this use of the term all believers are part of the Church whether they attend church or not. Indeed some who attend church may not be part of this mystical body. The various meanings which are associated with the word church can be confusing, but it does indicate not only the importance of the term for Christians, but also the possibility of a variety of interpretations as to what kind of group and activity should properly be called church. Despite this fact, for many Christians, church is a fairly clear term which denotes authenticity. The Church is characterized by the authorized and proper ministry of both word and sacraments. We go to church where we meet people with whom we share a set of beliefs and have fellowship.

While I see the real need for whatever we consider to be church to be well-defined, I would argue that our current thinking needs to be expanded a little. Indeed there is some evidence that in popular expression 'churchness' is wider than the definitions I have already mentioned. For example the word church is commonly used for relatively informal gatherings such as a house group. Some Christians who attend worship in a recognized church on a Sunday might express this kind of feeling by saying, 'I go to church but my home group is my real church.' There is something which we regard as being church about community groups. The same could be said of the many missionary activities which Christian people undertake. Work amongst the homeless or outreach projects are often regarded as an expression of the missionary concern of the Church. Thus we speak of these missionary projects as 'the Church reaching out to people'. I would therefore suggest that it is possible to regard Church as existing in three forms: missionary project, community group and as institution.[1]

The Church of the New Testament and of later periods has existed sequentially and simultaneously in these **three** forms. In many cases churches can trace their origins back through the gathering together of an informal group of believers and on to the establishment of a more formal organization. Some churches still have memories of the first missionary initiative which brought the original community group into existence. In the New Testament we see a similar progression where the missionary activity of someone such as Paul results in the formation of a community of believers. As time goes on these communities began to organize themselves developing specific ministries and rules of conduct for the whole group. Paul's letters to the church in Corinth are a good example of the way that this kind of ordering of the Church began to quite naturally evolve. Thus even in the New Testament we can see community groups which have been generated by missionary projects starting to institutionalize.

The sequential progression from missionary project to community group and then institution is well-accepted. The temptation is to see these as a hierarchical evolution thus one stage supersedes the other and renders the former obsolete. This is a mistake since it is also possible for these three aspects of church to coexist. Indeed I would argue that it is important that Church is expressed as institution, community group and missionary project in every town and locality.

THE CHURCH AS INSTITUTION

In recent times many Christians have sought to downplay or even try to avoid the institutional nature of the Church. Local churches, often under the influence of charismatic renewal, have sought to express their life in more communal rather than institutional forms. Fellowship and intimacy have been valued above organization and structure. Some Christians have self-consciously turned away from 'denominations' and formed their own fellowships and house churches. These developments have carried much which is good with them, yet there is a sense in which in seeking 'community' they have failed to appreciate the importance of the institutional characteristics of the Church. The institutional nature of the Church has six basic elements which make it essential to the pattern of the life of the people of God.

Tradition: It is the institutional nature of the Church which keeps the historic legacy of the Church alive. Those of us seeking new ways of being church with young people are increasingly turning for inspiration to the tradition of the Church. Thus many alternative worship services are using forms of worship which many would associate with the Catholic or Orthodox traditions. Without the Church as institution these traditions would be largely inaccessible. The tradition of the Church links us with Christians of previous generations and as such it is an important corrective to the tendency to be too closely linked to our particular cultural expression of the faith.

Longevity: Related to tradition, institutionalization is essential for social movements to ensure their survival. The informality of community groups means that they tend to burn themselves out. They avoid this by finding ways to routinize their leadership and community life.[2] Ironically what many have sought to renew in recent years – the regularized, habitual worship of the Church – has also been its strength. There is merit in the way that the Church has developed sustainable forms of worship and organization which are able to exist through the centuries. The Church exists for us now because these regularized patterns of life have withstood spiritual apathy as well as finding ways to slowly adapt and change in the light of spiritual enthusiasm. Our impatience with the Church as institution must to some extent be tempered by an admiration for its ability to endure.

Organization: Institutionalization is an inevitable result of success. Community groups need to regularize their life as time goes on and as they grow. Thus patterns of leadership, worship, finance and administration tend to become more organized. The same is true of relationships with other Christian groups and the wider society. These relationships, which quickly follow the establishment of a group, are essential not only to ministry but also to a sense of identity and acceptance. Relationships outside the community group demand a more formal means of communication and leadership. A very practical example of this would be the fact that most churches would be very keen to acquire charitable status and thus fulfil requirements of the Inland Revenue for reclaiming tax on covenants. This kind of advantageous development inevitably demands existence within the law and therefore a more organized structure.

Universality: The institutional nature of the Church reflects the gospel imperative of all Christians, of whatever racial or social group, in some sense being united in Christ. The institution of the Church is the means by which we keep alive the need for all Christians to be in association with each other.

Legitimacy: It is the institution of the Church through its leaders which alone is able to give legitimacy to both community groups and missionary projects. The institution is the means by which innovation is recognized and valued. An example of this would be the youth church Soul Survivor Watford which has been accepted as having an informal relationship with the Anglican Church by the Bishop of St Albans. Another would be the way that Cardinal Basil Hume has made a place within the Roman Catholic Church for the Upper Room, a charismatic community of young people.

Fellowship: The Church as institution should not be seen as a purely bureaucratic organization because it also has a relationship aspect to it. These relationships, however, are distinct from those which exist within the community group. Relationships within the institution have been regularized and ordered. An example of this is the way that home groups are planned by most churches. Such groups become part of the regular contact of the institution. They generally come about through the initiative of authorized leaders. Relationships within the institution, however, are relatively undemanding. A weekly attendance at a service or meeting can be regarded as sufficient 'commitment'. The community group in contrast emerges from 'below'. In the community group charismatic leaders come to the fore. The leader's authority is given by the members of the group rather than by the selection and training of the institution. The community group will often demand a much higher level of active involvement from members than that which exists in the institution. In some cases this might mean sharing a communal lifestyle or a common purse.

THE CHURCH AS COMMUNITY GROUP

Most churches can point to aspects of their life which are more akin to community groups, e.g. home groups or base communities. These community groups enrich the life of the institution giving it a focus and a cohesion which might otherwise be missing. A community group is often the place where people feel a sense of belonging and identity, but it can also be a forum for innovation and change. Community groups may reflect age, racial or social divisions within society. Thus a student Christian Union is in some respects a community group, as would be a women's group meeting to develop new liturgy. At times the relationship between the community groups and the institutional Church may be stormy. The community group may challenge the comfort zones of the institution. For its part the institution may feel threatened and try to close it down, or if that fails use more subtle means to undermine the legitimacy of the community group. A healthy and dynamic church, however, needs to exist as both institution and community groups. The two aspects of church need each other. The institution looks to community groups for energy and periodic refreshment. The community group needs the institution to provide a tradition to react against and renew.[3]

When the community group severs itself from the institution and sets out to become in and of itself a church, it soon finds itself institutionalized. At the same time community groups may find themselves taken over by the institution of the Church. One example of this would be the way that music and styles of worship which have originated within groups such as the Iona Community in Scotland have slowly begun to find their way into mainstream church life. This is the role of community groups – at first they are radical and innovative, but over a period of time their way of doing things can become accepted by the wider Church. The institution thus responds by slowly incorporating the life and energy of the community group. This is the way that community groups renew the

Church. If the community group does not continue to innovate and grow, its independence from the institution will become less important as the life and worship of mainstream church life reflects the values of the community group. Eventually the community group ceases to have a reason to exist and it withers away.

THE CHURCH AS MISSIONARY PROJECT

The missionary aspect of the Church involves a small number of individuals who make a conscious physical or cultural journey to reach out to a particular community or focus on a defined need in society. Christian work amongst the homeless would be a good example of this, or a Youth for Christ centre. The missionary group will be a committed and trained 'band' who set themselves apart from the main body of believers to prepare themselves for their chosen aspect of missionary service.[4] In many cases this missionary journey will involve them leaving their jobs behind or seeking paid support from the rest of the Church so that they can devote themselves to the task. The missionary project is essential because without it many aspects of the call of God upon the Church would go unheeded. The Church as institution and the Church as community group need the Church as missionary project. Not all church members are called to the same kinds of evangelistic or social service. The missionary project is the means by which the Church makes room for experimental work reaching beyond the formal structures of the institution. It is also distinctive because it generally involves an incarnational engagement beyond the social, racial or generational boundaries which characterize the community group. The missionary project is a prophetic witness to the rest of the Church that those in need and those who currently are outside the institution of the Church and community group are close to the heart of God.

Youth ministry must take the Church much more seriously. The problem for many youth ministers is that the institution of the Church in this country has attempted to locate all three aspects of the Church's life in its own structures. Local

123

churches have wanted to play down their institutionalized structures and emphasize fellowship and belonging. The net result of this has been that community groups linked to churches have been very closely controlled. Most of these groups are set up to serve institutional ends, rather than develop new forms of worship or social engagement. The spread of institution-sponsored groups has meant that genuine community groups find it hard to be accepted by the institution. One result of this has been that dissent and innovation have often been quashed. When community groups have been uncomfortable the tendency has been for churches to marginalize them. This has been the experience not only of some of those involved in alternative worship, it is also the experience of some women's groups. In this way the institutional Church has generally failed to maintain the dynamic relationship it should have with what might prove to be uncomfortable community groups. This results in it being extremely difficult to be 'owned' as part of a local, regional or national Church without totally fitting into the structures. This does not mean that there are no examples of positive relationships. The Upper Room in the Catholic Church and Soul Survivor Watford in the Anglican Church are proof of this, but these examples are comparatively few and far between. More often the existence of such groups has been discouraged as the local church has sought to be both institution and community group at the same time.

Similarly the local church in recent times has tended to see itself as the focus of missionary work in an area. The idea of independent missionary projects has been discouraged as churches have increased their staff numbers by appointing their own workers. The policy, particularly in youth ministry, has been for churches to try and cover both the needs of the children of Christian parents and some strategy for outreach in one appointment. This means that incarnational patterns of ministry have often been neglected. Churches feel they are doing their bit by employing a youth minister and therefore have a tendency to see no need to donate money to groups such as Frontier Youth Trust or Youth For Christ. The result of this has been a decline in some of these ministries and an

increasing sense of isolation amongst incarnational youthworkers.

If we accept that the Church can be seen as existing as institution, community group and missionary project, it follows
that some of the contemporary aspects of youth ministry can
be more readily accepted. In my understanding of Church
each of the three elements is itself church. At the same time
each element needs the others to be fully itself. The implication
of this is that a youth church could be recognized as truly
church. To be church, however, it does not have to be independent in its leadership or even its finances. To be fully church it
needs a relationship with the institution, since it is only the
institution which can bestow legitimate churchness. The consequence of my argument is that missionary projects are able to
remain independent from the institution of the Church, but
they must also build relationships. These relationships are
what guarantee their integrity as Church in missionary mode.
Of course the other side of the argument is that an institution
without relationships with community groups or missionary
projects is not fulfilling itself as church. It is the role of the
institution to seek both unity and diversity.

The threefold understanding of Church allows for generational groups to talk of themselves as church. It also allows
for the independent reality of such a community group based
on young people. It also accepts that certain church type
activities, e.g. the administration of the sacraments and
appointing of leaders, are a legitimate part of their life. These
things, however, need to be done in relationship with the
Church as institution. This may create problems for churches
such as the Anglican Church which has traditionally linked
unity and its own sense of identity to priesthood and the sacraments and located these in designated parishes or institutions,
e.g. schools and hospitals. The organization and the self-
understanding of the Anglican Church effectively denies true
churchness to community groups. Such a position will need
to be revised if the threefold understanding of the Church is
adopted. It is the role of the institution to find ways to adapt
to grass roots community initiatives. The spirit of being church

arises from the community life of the new group, but status and recognition come from the institution.

As far as the community is concerned, there is a need to work at relationship with the institution. The institution will at times favour caution over innovation, this must be received with understanding and perhaps resisted. At the same time the community will need help and guidance, this must be sought and accepted. The relationship between the institution and community will be at times stressful and extremely fragile. The temptation for the community will be to go it alone. This will often be a mistake. The success of any youth congregation or youth church will require the ability to walk the fine line between cautious inactivity and maverick creativity, between following the Spirit and sticking to the rules.

Creativity: A Sacramental Approach

Worship is both a divine encounter and a cultural activity. These two are intimately connected, you can't have one without the other. We experience God 'incarnated' within culture. Worship is similarly incarnational. The starting point for the development of worship which connects with the subcultures of young people is therefore the realization that worship is both a divine encounter and a social construction. Worship therefore has both human and divine elements. One way of thinking about the way human creativity and divine inspiration combine in worship is to use the language of sacrament. Theologically a sacrament is a sign or symbol of a deeper spiritual reality. For most Christians there is one defining sacrament seen in the bread and the wine of the Holy Communion service. The 'elements' of the bread and wine point beyond themselves to the fact that in some way during the worship service Christ comes and meets the believer. Definitions of how this comes about will vary from Catholic to more Protestant Christians but this kind of sacramental understanding is common to both. Holy Communion and baptism are recognized as sacraments, because in the scriptures God promises to meet us at these moments. The precise form of the ritual which makes up the sacrament varies according to culture and theological tradition. This means that Christians celebrate these two sacraments very differently, but we do so in the faith that however we frame the sacrament God's Spirit will come and honour us within our worship. Some churches have traditionally added to the number of sacraments by including confirmation, confession, marriage, ordination and the anointing of the sick.[5] In more recent times sacramental thinking has been used to offer an understanding of how we encounter God in the normal circumstances of life. For Leonardo Boff a sacrament is a much more ordinary reality. It is a thing from this world which evokes something from a different reality. In this way everyday items can become signs or symbols.[6]

A sacramental understanding of worship is vital for a contextual approach to work amongst young people. If worship is sacramental then it is possible to see that there might be a number of cultural forms for worship within which God might encounter different groups of people. It is a regular temptation for the Church to become identified with only one subculture or culture. At the heart of this is the genuine spiritual energy and encounter with God which many Christians experience in church worship. The problem comes, however, when God's presence is linked to a particular style of music or liturgy. Real encounter with God leads to the baptism of a style of worship which is itself contextualized in culture. The use of a sacramental understanding should caution youthworkers and clergy against this kind of problem.

The aim of youth ministry should be to set free the cultural creativity of young people in worship. Youth culture has its own subcultural expressions of celebration, lamentation and community life. These indigenous cultural elements should become the building blocks for a new expression of worship and church life. A sacramental understanding of encounter between God and humanity offers a framework for understanding how the culture of young people and the work of the Holy Spirit may coincide.

Worship and Meaning Making

Meaning and worship are integrally related. Worship helps us to create and maintain a sense of meaning. It is as we meet with God that we start to develop some order out of the randomness of life. Worship helps us to work through pain and grief. The experience of life might at times bring confusion and doubt, yet worship offers a sense that God is still at work. One of the ways that we experience this in worship is through storytelling. Worship is the occasion where the people of God rehearse the story of the gospel. In telling the story we also search for our own place within the narrative. In short we engage in meaning making.

The story of the gospel gives meaning by offering a sense of identity. When we are able to locate ourselves within the overarching activity of God, we see more clearly who we are. The gospel gives us a sense of meaning because our encounter with God means that we are 'seen' in a new light. We are a new creation, children of the same heavenly parent, people called to share in the mission of God, those with the secret of the kingdom. Our identity is therefore intimately related to the status that comes to us because of what Jesus has done for us on the cross. The good news is that in the death of Christ we understand that God regards us as being incredibly valuable. When we tell the story of the gospel in worship, we recall the worth that God gives to us. This is why the words of the liturgy, songs, and most importantly of the Bible, give us a sense of dignity and self-worth. We build meaning in worship because as we rehearse the gospel we understand our place in relation to God. It is our relationship to God which gives us a framework for understanding ourselves, but it also links us to a wider Christian community.

The gospel story builds a sense of being church. Individual encounter with God has implications for a wider community life. Our relationship with God means that we are also in relation with every other Christian of whatever age, race or gender. It is God who links us into a body of believers who depend upon one another. The Christian experience is in many respects counter-cultural because it transcends cultural barriers. This does not mean that all culture is nullified or lacks importance. It simply means that we carry with us our culture into a wider fellowship of all believers. When Christians meet to worship we are acting as a sign of this more universal allegiance. At the same time we do so by using particular cultural expressions, musical forms, rituals and behaviours. Our sense of who we are as Christians is built from regular community involvement. It may be that weekly fellowship will be primarily with those who share an appreciation for one style of worship expressed in distinctive cultural forms which ring true. Our sense of who we are is formed by this kind of commitment to seek and to be sought by God together. Christian unity across national and cultural boundaries is also expressed by the Church acting as institution. Our identity as Christians within the wider Church and the local setting rests therefore on both the institutional and the community aspects of the Church's existence.

The community meeting to worship week by week reinforces a particular view of the world. There is no one Christian worldview. Instead there are communities of Christians who share a way of looking at things. The community perspective on life is generated by a creative reading of the gospel story in the light of social, political and moral issues. Walter Brueggemann speaks of praise as a God-given duty, an act of liturgical imagination where we suspend business as usual. In praise we embrace hope and an alternative future. According to Brueggemann, 'Praise not only celebrates God but portrays the world given us by this God now received as sovereign.'[7] Worship is world making an interaction between the culture of the community and the sovereign nature of God. How these are merged is a creative contextualization, the culture of the community being the medium within which God is sacramentally present. We should expect the presence of God to both affirm our culture by making himself known within it, and to challenge us to kingdom lifestyles.

Worship is not only the place where these values are worked out but it is also the means whereby what is essentially a contextualized approach to Christian living is repeated. We express our new identity within culture through sermons, discussion, the words of hymns or songs, and the words used in liturgy. Those who join the worship of the community are socialized into these values. However, it is possible for individuals to assent to some of the values of the group, but at the same time maintain independence by developing forms of informal resistance to them, e.g. disagreeing with the sermon over Sunday lunch. While some diversity will be possible within the community, radical dissent either results in a change in the corporate values or in individuals or small groups looking for a more congenial community to belong to. On the whole the worldview associated with the community will be more or less held in common by the Christians who meet together. As such it generates a structure of meaning by giving a shared worldview through which to interpret life. This worldview arises from the interaction of the cultural experience of the group with the tradition of the Church and the Bible. The construction of a worldview is a creative act, but it is also sacramental in that it is an attempt to seek the mind of God in building a meaningful life.

Sacred Space

When we worship we enter a set of social relationships and behaviours which we recognize as sacred. The experience of taking the collection or reading in church or of an open prayer time have left most of us at times feeling 'strange' or uncomfortable. This sense is an indication that we are entering the sacred space of ritual behaviour. There are many ways in which sacred or ritual space is signified. These include: sacred buildings set aside for worship, particular forms of music, a set of ritual postures, ways of speaking and listening, the use of the visual arts, special movements and actions, and distinctive ways of dressing.

Sacred space is a way of framing a different kind of reality. Ritual moves us into a new social arena which is open-ended towards God. According to Mary Douglas 'ritual provides a frame. The marked off time or place alerts a special kind of expectancy, just as the oft repeated "Once upon a time" creates a mood receptive to fantastic tales.'[8] Sacred space is a cultural creation. Humans make rituals within which we are expectant of meeting God. Protestants have been somewhat suspicious of ritual tending to regard 'ritualistic worship' as lacking meaning. This critique, however, is only part of the story, for the power of ritual lies to some extent in its ability to effect changes upon us and within us without our complete comprehension. Burying a close friend or relative is a profound experience, but at the same time there is a sense that the 'ritual' carries you through. It is possible to feel somewhat numb from grief and yet also to experience profound change towards both your own life and the life of the person to whom you are saying goodbye. The ritual of marriage can also be very powerful, but in unexpected ways. The experience of getting married is an event between the two people involved, but it is also extremely significant for those who attend. To be married is to be accepted in a new status by the wider community. A wedding in the 'face of this congregation' enables this kind of change to take place.

Ritual is also deeply cultural. Anthropologists, such as Douglas, have for some time studied the ritualistic behaviours of different groups of people. Christian ritual is also cultural and young people who are creating worship for themselves will need to establish ways of worshipping ritualistically which are appropriate within their own subcultural setting. Of course youth culture itself comes with numerous ritualistic behaviours – dance, dress, greeting, performance and language all hold a power for young people. Christian worship contextualized within popular culture will transform these existing ritualistic forms of behaviour with a sacramental theology. Some aspects of the existing rituals will need to be abandoned in the light of the gospel story, others however may be seen as helpful for Christian worship, e.g. the use of popular forms of dance or music.

Imagination, Risk and Play

Creativity can be something of a mystery. We hear a good piece of music, or we look at a painting, or we read a novel and there is a part of each of us which is in awe. Most of us have asked the question, 'How could we ever create something as clever or beautiful as this?' We consume the creative products of other people, but in so doing there is often a sense in which our consumption of the cultural products is alienating us from our own ability to create. There is a widespread loss of imagination in adult life. Part of the reason for this is that the creativity of professional 'artists' can leave us feeling wanting in our own skills or abilities. The other side of this is that it is a good deal easier to play a worship song written by someone else than it is to write our own. Consumption of other people's creativity can be a form of convenience religion.

The problem for young people and youthworkers seeking to develop contextualized worship is that creativity is essential. The worship which exists in the Church in its current form is largely unhelpful because it has been shaped by the cultural sensitivities of the people who currently attend church. This means that we need to find ways to express worship in words, songs, rituals and community life which ring true within the subculture of the group of which we are a part.

Imagination and creativity do not come out of thin air. While some people are 'gifted', it is also true to say that each of us has the ability to create in some way or another. It is salutary and encouraging to realize that all artists have to work at their craft. Moreover they do not create out of thin air. It is only God who creates from nothing. The rest of us create from things which already exist. A journey through an art gallery illustrates these two points very well. It is possible to see how one artist after another has drawn inspiration and has created something new from the creativity of those who went before them. The same is true of music where particular musical steps forward can be seen as the merging of previously known styles. An example of this is the way that rock and roll was created by drawing on the already existing styles of gospel, blues and country music. Within the work of particular artists, it is possible to see how the creative process takes place. The development of work in Picasso where he is seen to move from one 'period' to another, or the way that Van Gogh would work with particular subjects to find the right way of expressing what he was seeing. Most of the rest of us would be happy with one picture of sunflowers, but Van Gogh repeated this picture again and again. His art was worked on over a period of time using trial and error as the means to achieve the effect he was seeking at the time.

The same kind of thing can be seen in the work of a contemporary band such as Oasis, where some of the early material shows signs of particular musical phrases which are repeated in the later songs. The early songs are at best fairly average, but the same phrase when used in a later song contributes to a sublime musical moment. Bob Dylan does a similar thing at times using exactly the same tune to write a new lyric. The one song is recognized as being amazing, but the other can remain comparatively unknown.

Creativity involves a process of developing the imagination. This happens through merging new ways of looking at things with other, older modes of expression. The overall result, if everything goes to plan, is a move forward. This takes place largely through a process of trial and error. The artist creates something and then takes a step back to try and assess how it looks. With what has been learned, hopefully, the next time something better can be achieved. There is therefore a good deal of perspiration in being creative as well as a small grain of inspiration.

The sacramental view of life will assert that this creative process is one which is charged with the presence of God. The Christian artist is one who is seeking God by the exercise of a Spirit-filled imagination. Where artistic creations are to be used in worship the desire is that God will become present to the whole community through them. Creativity in worship is linked to the need for worship to be meaningful and meaning making for the Christian community. Imagination is a basic element in this contextualized approach to creativity in worship.

One way of understanding imagination is to look at the way that children use play as a way to understand the world. Jerome Berryman in dealing with the education of young children points out the importance of play as a means of creating meaning. He calls this 'Godly play'.[9] He explains that,

> Godly play is the playing of a game that can awaken us to new ways of seeing ourselves as human beings. It is the way to discover our deep identity as Godly creatures, created in the image of God. The possibility of Godly play puts

133

the games played for glory, fame and wealth, even for salvation into a new and astounding frame. This larger frame, staked out at the limits of our being and knowing, reveals how limited the other games are and how they turn play into work so that the player winds down into self-destruction.

Godly play for Berryman involves working with spiritual issues in the light of sacred symbols and stories. When young people begin to construct worship for themselves, symbols are used to make sense of this experience.

Most new worship services run by young people are experimenting with liturgy which uses a number of different media. Music and visual art as well as ritual are being explored in new ways. This area is covered in much more detail in *Worship and Youth Culture*,[10] for the present discussion, however, the key point is that contextualized worship comes about when young people make their own sacred space by drawing on elements from within their own subculture and on the more traditional aspects of Christian worship. Godly play describes the way that popular culture and Christian tradition are worked with to create something which is located within the life of a particular community. The point of play is that although this is a serious activity, it has an element of experiment about it.

Play is a metaphor for the way that creativity can be developed in worship. New forms of worship contextualized in youth culture come about when we combine one symbol from popular culture with another from the biblical material, e.g. a picture of a Coke bottle with the story of Jesus turning over the money-changers' tables in the temple, or the picture of a terrorist with the celebration of the Holy Communion. Play involves trying something out to see how it feels or looks. This process inevitably involves some risk. There will be times when we get it wrong. The use of the term 'play', however, gives a lightness of touch to the process in which we are engaged. This is completely opposite to the way that the Anglican Church, for instance, revises its liturgy. In the Church of England the usual approach to liturgical revision involves setting up committees to slowly deliberate on the creation of a universal liturgy which will be authorized by General Synod for use in the Church. Thus the Church is cautious and tries to eliminate risk. By contrast, play sees worship as an arena for taking risks and occasionally getting things wrong. The appropriate response when things fall apart is to laugh, learn from the mistake and do it better next time, just as young children will occasionally bump themselves or fall over trying to learn a new dance step or playing football. Godly play is serious, but it is also good fun. Our task as youthworkers should be to enable young people to encounter God as sovereign in worship. In doing this they bring their own culture and identity and find it transformed by God's presence and perspective.

Notes

Chapter 1

1 By 'traditions' I mean the historic practices of youthwork; 'disciplines' are the methodologies which happen within those practices.

2 See the work of Frontier Youth Trust, in particular Terry Dunnell, *Mission and Young People at Risk*, FYT, 1985.

3 See Jon Langford, 'Let's Get Spiritual' in *Young People Now* (June 1994); and Martin Shaw, 'Religious Development' in *Young People Now* (June 1994).

4 For more on this, see Pete Ward, *Growing up Evangelical*, SPCK, 1996.

5 For more on ideal types, see 'Ideal Type' in David Jary and Julia Jary, *Dictionary of Sociology*, Collins, 1991.

6 I first saw this illustration in a training leaflet produced by Mark Ashton when he was head of Church Youth Fellowship Association.

7 Tricia Williams, *Christians in School*, Scripture Union, 1985, p. 14.

8 An example of this position would be Mark Ashton and Phil Moon, *Christian Youthwork*, Monarch, 1995.

9 See *Christian Youthwork*.

10 For a historical perspective on this, see *Growing up Evangelical*, pp. 23ff.

11 See Bob Mayo, *Gospel Exploded*, Triangle, 1996.

12 See *Growing up Evangelical*, pp. 63ff.

13 See Mark Smith, *Developing Youthwork*, Open University, 1988, pp. 1ff; and Kathleen Heaseman, *Evangelicals in Action*, Geoffrey Bles, 1962.

14 By using the term 'incarnational' in this way, I do not mean to imply that only those who work outside-in are following the example of Jesus. The ministry of adults and young people in a nucleus group is equally an imitation of Christ. I use the term therefore in a technical way as it is commonly used in missiology to denote the crossing of barriers to share the faith by being with a group of people.

15 See Roger Sainsbury, *From a Mersey Wall*, Scripture Union, 1970; and Peter Stow, *Youth in the City*, Hodder and Stoughton, 1987.

16 See Pip Wilson, *Gutter Feelings*, Hodder and Stoughton, 1985.

17 *Growing up Evangelical*, pp. 199ff.

18 Charles Kraft, *Christianity in Culture*, Orbis, 1984, p. 5.

19 For more on this, see Chapter 7.

20 I can't imagine that Clucas has ever written this down, but I am sure that

he will be more than happy to explain his ideas at length if you care to call him at Church Pastoral Aid Society.

21 I confess I have been guilty of this in the past.

Chapter 2

1 See 'A Theology for Youthwork' in *Youth Apart*, Church House, 1996. I am indebted to Graham Cray, who played a large part in developing the theology sections of *Youth Apart*, for many of the insights in this chapter.

2 A rendering of John 20.27.

3 See Jürgen Moltmann, *The Crucified God*, SCM Press, 1974, p. 243.

4 Dean Borgman 'Youth, Culture, and Media: Contemporary Youth Ministry' in *Transformation*, Vol. 11, No. 2 (April/June 1994), p. 13.

5 For more on this, see Frances Young, *Sacrifice and the Death of Christ*, SCM Press, 1975.

6 'Redemption' in Alan Richardson and John Bowden (eds), *A New Dictionary of Christian Theology*, SCM Press, 1983.

7 The Alternative Service Book, 1980.

8 Isaac Watts, 'When I survey the Wondrous Cross'. This hymn and others are used by Frances Young in *Sacrifice and the Death of Christ*.

9 See Karl Barth, *The Epistle to the Romans*, Oxford University Press, 1933.

10 See *Epistle to the Romans*.

11 See Alister McGrath, *Evangelicalism and the Future of Christianity*, Hodder and Stoughton, 1995, pp. 137ff.

12 Edward Schillebeeckx, *Jesus*, Fount, 1979, pp. 206ff; also Joachim Jeremias, *New Testament Theology: Volume One*, SCM Press, 1971, pp. 118ff.

13 Used by kind permission of Anna Chakka George and Fiona Macleod.

14 This point was suggested to me by David Howell.

Chapter 3

1 Different employers have differing guidelines. The voluntary agencies have a duty to try to ensure that youthwork is 'safe'. Good advice and guidelines are generally available from the Anglican Diocesan Youth Officers.

2 For more on this, see Pete Ward, Sam Adams and Jude Levermore, *Youthwork and How to Do it*, Lynx, 1994, pp. 21ff; also Pete Ward, 'Christian Relational Care' in Pete Ward (ed.), *Relational Youthwork*, Lynx, 1995.

3 This is a phrase I first heard from Arnie Jacobs of Young Life who inspired me and a number of others to try and do youthwork better.

4 For more on this, contact Steve Connor at Christians in Sport, P.O. Box 93, Oxford.

5 For more on communication with young people, see Jude Levermore's excellent chapter in *Youthwork and How to Do it*.

6 The Manor is Oxford United's football ground.

7 See Jude Levermore's chapter in *Youthwork and How to Do it*.

8 For more on Jim Rayburn, see Jim Rayburn III, *Dance Children Dance*, Tyndale, 1984; also Mark Senter, *The Coming Revolution in Youth Ministry*, Victor Books, 1992, pp. 17ff.

9 I have said a little more on this topic in Pete Ward, *Youth Culture and the Gospel*, HarperCollins, 1992; and Pete Ward, *Worship and Youth Culture*, HarperCollins, 1993.

10 See *Gospel Exploded*.

11 These matters are dealt with at length in Chapters 5 and 6.

12 See Phil Moon, *Hanging in There*, Monarch, 1994, p. 58.

13 For an alternative approach to this which combines contact work with a nucleus group, see Mark Senter, 'Emerging Patterns of Youth Ministry at the End of the Century' in *Relational Youthwork*.

Chapter 4

1 Much of what follows in this chapter is based on Jim McGuigan *Cultural Populism*, Routledge, 1992; and Mike Brake, *Comparative Youth Culture*, Routledge, Kegan and Paul, 1985.

2 *Comparative Youth Culture*, p. 2.

3 See Louis J. Luzbetak, *The Church and Cultures*, Orbis, 1988, pp. 12ff.

4 Richard Hoggart, *The Uses of Literacy*, Chatto and Windus, 1957; E.P. Thompson, *The Making of the English Working Class*, Victor Gollancz, 1963; Raymond Williams, *Culture and Society*, Chatto and Windus, 1958.

5 Ian Davies, *Cultural Studies and Beyond*, Routledge, 1995, pp. 35ff.

6 *Comparative Youth Culture*, p. 3.

7 Stuart Hall and Tony Jefferson, *Resistance through Rituals*, Hutchinson, 1975, pp. 5ff.

8 Angela McRobbie and Mica Nava (eds), *Gender and Generation*, Macmillan, 1984; and Angela McRobbie, *Feminism and Youth Culture: From Jackie to Just Seventeen*, Macmillan, 1991.

9 Dick Hebdige, *Subculture: The Meaning of Style*, Methuen, 1979.

10 Paul Corrigan, 'Doing Nothing' in *Resistance through Rituals*.

11 Peter Marsh, Elizabeth Rosser and Rom Harré, *The Rules of Disorder*, Routledge, Kegan and Paul, 1978.

12 Q. Schultze, R. Anker, J. Bratt, W. Romanowski, J. Worst and L. Zuidervaart, *Dancing in the Dark*, Eerdmans, 1991.

13 Neil Postman, *Amusing Ourselves to Death*, Penguin, 1985.

14 John Buckeridge in *Youthwork* (August/September 1992).

15 For more on this, see *Growing up Evangelical*.

16 Paul Willis, *Common Culture*, Open University, 1990, pp. 1ff.
17 *Common Culture*, pp. 9ff.
18 John Fiske, *Understanding Popular Culture*, Routledge, 1989, pp. 28ff.
19 *Understanding Popular Culture*, p. 24.
20 *Common Culture*, p. 13.
21 *Common Culture*, p. 13.
22 *Common Culture*, pp. 141–5.
23 See *Cultural Populism*.
24 Andrew Walker, *Telling the Story*, SPCK, 1996.

Chapter 5

1 See *Youth Culture and the Gospel*.
2 For more on dynamic equivalents translation, see *Christianity in Culture*.
3 Karl Barth 'The Strange New World Within the Bible' in *The Word of God and the Word of Man*, Hodder and Stoughton, 1928.
4 Eugene Peterson, *The Message*, NavPress, 1994; Walter Wangerin, *The Book of God*, Lion, 1996.
5 Dietrich Bonhoeffer, *The Cost of Discipleship*, SCM Press, 1948.

Chapter 6

1 For more on this, see *Sacrifice and the Death of Christ*.
2 *Telling the Story*, pp. 12ff.
3 *New Testament Theology: Volume One*, p. 118.
4 *Jesus*, p. 206.
5 Tony Campolo, *The Church and the American Teenager*, Zondervan, 1989, pp. 32ff.
6 Based on a personal conversation with Tony Campolo.
7 I am indebted to the work of successive groups of Oxford Youth Works students for these two case studies. As presented these are composite pictures based on a number of student presentations.

Chapter 7

1 This is based on a combination of the ecclesial typology of Ernst Troeltsch in *The Social Teaching of the Christian Churches*, George Allen, 1931 and Ralph Winter, 'The Two Structures of God's Redemptive Mission' in *Missiology* (January 1974). For an earlier treatment of Winter, see Pete Ward, 'Distance and Closeness' in Pete Ward (ed.), *The Church and Youth Ministry*, Lynx, 1995.
2 See H. H. Gerth and C. Wright Mills, *Essays from Max Weber*, Routledge, 1948, pp. 262ff.
3 These insights are based on Leonardo Boff, *Ecclesiogenesis*, Collins, 1986;

Notes

and Rosemary Radford Ruether, *Women-Church*, Harper and Row, 1985.

See 'The Two Structures of God's Redemptive Mission'.

See 'Sacramental Theology' in *A New Dictionary of Christian Theology*.

See Leonardo Boff, *Sacraments of Life, Life of the Sacraments*, The Pastoral Press, 1987.

Walter Brueggemann, *Israel's Praise*, Fortress, 1988, p. 49.

Mary Douglas, *Purity and Danger*, Ark, 1984, p. 63.

Jerome W. Berryman, *Godly Play*, HarperCollins, 1991, p. 7.

Pete Ward, *Worship and Youth Culture*, HarperCollins, 1993.

The Society for Promoting Christian Knowledge (SPCK) has as its purpose three main tasks:

- **Communicating the Christian faith in its rich diversity**
- **Helping people to understand the Christian faith and to develop their personal faith**
- **Equipping Christians for mission and ministry**

SPCK Worldwide serves the Church through Christian literature and communication projects in over 100 countries. Special schemes also provide books for those training for ministry in many parts of the developing world. SPCK Worldwide's ministry involves Churches of many traditions. This worldwide service depends upon the generosity of others and all gifts are spent wholly on ministry programmes, without deductions.

SPCK Bookshops support the life of the Christian community by making available a full range of Christian literature and other resources, and by providing support to bookstalls and book agents throughout the UK. SPCK Bookshops' mail order department meets the needs of overseas customers and those unable to have access to local bookshops.

SPCK Publishing produces Christian books and resources, covering a wide range of inspirational, pastoral, practical and academic subjects. Authors are drawn from many different Christian traditions, and publications aim to meet the needs of a wide variety of readers in the UK and throughout the world.

The Society does not necessarily endorse the individual views contained in its publications, but hopes they stimulate readers to think about and further develop their Christian faith.

For further information about the Society, please write to:
SPCK, Holy Trinity Church, Marylebone Road,
London NW1 4DU, United Kingdom.
Telephone: 0171 387 5282